STUDENT UNIT GUIDE

NEW EDITION

Edexcel AS Government & Politics
Unit 1
People and Politics

Paul Cordey

Editors: Eric Magee and Neil McNaughton

Philip Allan Updates, an imprint of Hodder Education, an Hachette UK company, Market Place, Deddington, Oxfordshire OX15 0SE

Orders
Bookpoint Ltd, 130 Milton Park, Abingdon, Oxfordshire OX14 4SB
tel: 01235 827827
fax: 01235 400401
e-mail: education@bookpoint.co.uk
Lines are open 9.00 a.m.–5.00 p.m., Monday to Saturday, with a 24-hour message answering service. You can also order through the Philip Allan Updates website: www.philipallan.co.uk

ISBN 978-1-4441-4812-1

First printed 2011
Impression number 5 4
Year 2015 2014 2013 2012

Printed in Dubai

Hachette UK's policy is to use papers that are natural, renewable and recyclable products and made from wood grown in sustainable forests. The logging and manufacturing processes are expected to conform to the environmental regulations of the country of origin.

P01925

Contents

Content Guidance

Questions & Answers

Getting the most from this book

Questions & Answers

Exam-style questions

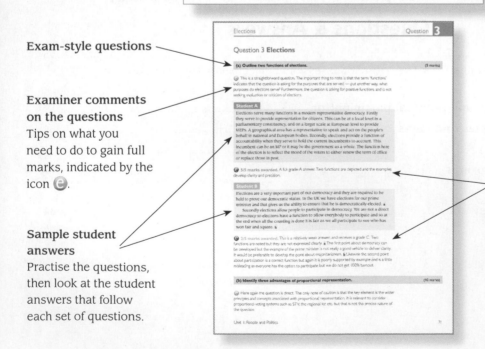

About this book

This guide is for students following the Edexcel AS Government and Politics course. It aims to guide you through Unit 1: People and Politics.

The **Content Guidance** section provides a detailed guide to the four topic areas: Democracy and political participation, Party policies and ideas, Elections, and Pressure groups.

The **Questions & Answers** section provides examples of examination questions with student responses at different grades, together with examiner comments.

Content guidance

About this section

This part of the book presents the key knowledge, understanding and analysis that you will need to master the topics that will enable you to answer examination questions comprehensively. You will also find regular information about key concepts. Examiner tips are provided to help you avoid mistakes and to advise you on vital information to include in particular answers.

From time to time there is a knowledge check. Here you are invited to test various key aspects of your knowledge. These checks are numbered and, at the end of the guide, you can find suggested answers. You can then see how well you did in recalling the key information.

Democracy and political participation

What is democracy?

In general, democracy refers to any society and/or political system in which the people are able to make or influence decisions and where government is accountable to the people. More precise definitions would include the following:

- The word is derived from the Greek words *demos* and *kratis*, broadly meaning 'rule by the people'.
- Abraham Lincoln, the American president from 1861 to 1865, described democracy as 'government of the people, by the people, for the people'.

The modern, widely accepted meaning of democracy has a number of variations. These include direct democracy, representative democracy, liberal democracy, pluralist democracy. These overlap a great deal. Each is described in more detail below.

The UK, the USA and France are important examples of democratic states.

What is legitimacy?

Legitimacy is an idea that is very closely associated with democracy. In general, it means this:

> The idea that a government or any other political institution has a democratic right to hold political power

Democracy
A particular type of political system that involves, to varying degrees, citizen participation. Common principles are that decisions are reached after open discussion and debate on political activity, that government is accountable to the people and that there is a free flow of information. Many modern states aspire to or claim democratic status.

Legitimacy The principle that a regime, institution or individual has a legitimate right to exercise power. Legitimacy is usually, though not always, bestowed through election. The legitimacy of regimes or political bodies may be disputed.

Legitimacy is a contestable term in that it is not always clear whether an institution is legitimate. The following list of circumstances illustrates both the meaning of legitimacy and the problems in determining whether legitimacy is justified. Each case relates to the UK.

- The House of Commons is legitimate because it is elected. However, many claim that the electoral system is unfair and distorts political representation, so legitimacy can be challenged.
- The House of Lords is arguably not legitimate because its members are not elected. However, it does have traditional authority and its political influence remains widely recognised.
- UK government is legitimate because it is elected with a clear mandate to govern. However, every government in the UK has been elected with a minority of the popular vote, so we can challenge its legitimacy.
- The power of the prime minister is legitimate because it is widely acknowledged that he (or she) is the supreme policy maker in the political system. However, there is no legal basis for prime ministerial power, so it could be said to lack legitimacy.

If we look at other regimes we can see that legitimacy can be challenged even more strongly. For example:

- Regimes that seize power by force are not considered to be legitimate. This applies to the government of Cuba, where the communist party came to power after a civil war.
- States which have one-party systems, such as China, lack democratic legitimacy even though they might receive widespread popular support.
- States where democracy is considered to be a facade or 'sham' lack legitimacy. Iran is an example.
- Hereditary monarchies such as Saudi Arabia or Bahrain lack democratic legitimacy.

What is direct democracy?

The term 'direct democracy' effectively means two things:

1 The people themselves make important decisions rather than leaving decision making to elected or appointed representatives.
2 The people are directly involved in political decision making. This suggests they are consulted and their opinions are sought regularly.

Types of direct democracy

There are a number of ways in which direct democracy is used in modern democracies.

Referendums

A referendum is the most common form of direct democracy. The characteristics of referendums are as follows:

- A referendum occurs when an important decision is put to the people, rather than being determined by government and/or representative assemblies. It involves a single question where the answer is either 'yes' or 'no'.
- A referendum may be national or regional or local. Examples of each are shown in Table 3, p. 11.
- In some countries, referendum results are legally binding on government.

Knowledge check I
Consider each of the following British political institutions and decide whether they are legitimate and why: the monarchy, the House of Lords, the House of Commons, the prime minister.

Direct democracy
A description of a type or style of democracy where the people make important political decisions or are consulted before key decisions are made.

- In the UK the results of referendums are not binding on government or Parliament. This is because Parliament is sovereign. However, it is almost unthinkable that Parliament would overturn a referendum decision.

Initiatives

Initiatives occur most famously in some states of the USA, such as California, but are rare in the UK and have only been held at a very local level. An initiative is when groups of interested citizens organise a petition on a specific issue. If enough people sign, the government is forced to hold a referendum on the issue. The point here is that it is the people who have taken the initiative, rather than government itself.

Public consultations

It is increasingly the case that governments at various levels carry out a public consultation before making important decisions. Local authorities, for example, often ask the community how they would prefer funds to be allocated between different services. Central government too is increasingly using this device. The internet makes such exercises easier.

Petitions

Although petitions are not binding, they may be influential. Large numbers of citizens may sign a petition on a particular issue. In the UK Parliament, such petitions are not often debated or influential. In the Scottish Parliament, however, there is a special committee to consider such petitions and the more supported ones have to be debated by the whole Parliament and have some impact on Scottish government. Here again, the internet makes such petitions more feasible.

Direct democracy evaluated

Table 1 identifies the main arguments in favour of and against the use of direct democracy.

Table 1 The advantages and disadvantages of direct democracy

Advantages	Disadvantages
It is the purest form of democracy	Direct democracy means **majoritarianism** — government by a simple majority. This may represent the 'tyranny of the majority', which oppresses minorities
It disperses power widely among the population and so prevents a concentration of power in too few hands	
It means that decisions may be more acceptable to the population	Many decisions may be too complex for the people to understand
It can prevent decision makers from making mistakes	Direct democracy often creates an emotional, rather than a rational, response from the people and the media
It increases popular participation and therefore enhances democracy	Direct democracy can be subverted or distorted by wealthy groups who influence the debate
Referendums and consultations are a form of political education for the general population	
Referendums can 'entrench' or safeguard important constitutional changes	If required to participate too much, the population may become politically 'fatigued' and apathy will grow

Knowledge check 2

Prepare notes for an evaluation of direct democracy. What are the positive and negative aspects of direct democracy? Include examples and illustrations to support the analysis.

Examiner tip

Always try to give real-world examples when describing concepts such as legitimacy, direct democracy or representation.

What is representative democracy?

Representative democracy is the 'normal' model in modern states. In essence it means that the people elect, and sometimes appoint, individuals to act on their behalf, to be their political representatives. Representative democracies normally have the following features:

- There are free elections to representative assemblies.
- Elected representatives can be made accountable in various ways to the electorate.
- There is a legislature, part of whose role is to represent the people.
- Governments and heads of state are elected by the people.
- There are political parties to represent different political beliefs or various sections of the community.
- Political associations and pressure groups operate freely and represent various causes, beliefs and interest groups.

Representative democracy
A description of a type of democracy in which most decisions are made by representative bodies which are appointed or elected. There are strong representative institutions, accountable to the people. This type of democracy is in contrast to direct democracy.

Representative democracy evaluated

Table 2 The advantages and disadvantages of representative democracy

Advantages	Disadvantages
Elected or appointed representatives may have superior experience and judgement to the general population	Representatives may not accurately represent the opinions and demands of the wider population
Representatives are more likely to make rational judgements than the population, who may be swayed by emotion	Party representation in particular can prevent elected representatives from acting independently
Representatives are usually accountable, which helps to make them behave responsibly	Representative democracy can turn into 'rule by elites' rather than dispersed power, which occurs in direct democracy
The people cannot be continuously involved in politics and so can delegate their power to representatives	Representative democracy is only 'fair' if elections are also 'fair'
Representatives can mediate between the interests of different sections of society. This avoids the 'tyranny of the majority'	

Knowledge check 3

What are the key distinctions between direct democracy and representative democracy?

Representative democracy in the UK

The UK is considered to be a representative democracy. Most decisions are made by representatives rather than by direct democracy. The following features of **representation** exist in the UK:

- There are regular free elections. Virtually all adults can vote or stand for office. (It is arguable whether UK elections to Westminster are 'fair', given the first-past-the-post electoral system that distorts party representation.)
- There are elected representative assemblies at every level — national (the UK Parliament's House of Commons), regional (the Scottish Parliament and Welsh and Northern Ireland assemblies) and local (councils).
- Parties are free to operate and represent various political opinions.
- Political associations and pressure groups are free to operate and campaign and have access to government.

Representation
A political process whereby the people do not make decisions directly, but elect or appoint representatives to make decisions on their behalf. It implies that representatives make themselves accountable to Parliament or the people. It can also mean that institutions are socially representative of the whole community.

- Governments at all levels are accountable to representative assemblies.
- Every individual is represented by an MP, a regional assembly member and a local councillor, who may take up an individual's grievances in government.
- Every locality is also represented through the constituency responsibilities of MPs.

Critical evaluation of representative democracy in the UK

Although the UK is usually characterised as a representative democracy and displays many positive features, critics argue that it is not as representative as it might be. Among the criticisms are the following:

- Elections to the UK Parliament are unfair, with some parties over-represented (especially Labour) and some under-represented (Liberal Democrats).
- The House of Lords has considerable power, but is not elected. Its members are either appointed (life peers and bishops) or are hereditary peers (92 in number).
- Governments are not truly representative as they are always elected with a minority of the electorate's votes. The 2005–10 Labour government, for example, was elected on only 35% of the popular vote, (though the 2010 coalition did claim the support of 55% of the voters).
- Smaller parties, such as the Green Party or UKIP, are under-represented because of the electoral system.
- Some pressure groups are more powerful than others and their power and influence does not always reflect their size or popularity.
- It can be argued that government is not accountable enough. Parliament has many structural weaknesses in calling government to account, while local and regional elections are often fought on national, rather than regional or local issues.

Referendums in the UK

Why referendums have been held

The question here is: why have referendums been held rather than having issues determined by government and/or Parliament? Referendums have been used in the UK for the following reasons:

- Sometimes government itself is divided on an issue. In order to resolve the question, therefore, government may call a referendum to give the people the final say. Government can thus escape from its problem.
- It is now established as a **convention** (an unwritten constitutional principle) that any important constitutional change can only be made if approved by a referendum.
- Similarly, a referendum has the effect of entrenching a constitutional change, preventing it from being reversed too easily by a future government.
- It may be especially important to secure the consent of the community to a key change, especially if it may have implications for tax.

Pressure group An association, which may be formal or very loose, of people who campaign to further the interests of a section of society or to pursue a particular cause. Pressure groups campaign both within government and among the public, and may offer candidates for election. However, they do not seek governmental power, but rather to influence decision makers.

Referendum A vote conducted nationally, regionally or locally where the electorate is invited to determine a key political issue. A referendum focuses on a single question with a yes/no answer. The results of referendums are considered binding on representative institutions.

Examiner tip

When asked to describe the 'circumstances' of a referendum in the UK, you are expected to explain not just the nature of the question and its outcome, but also the *reasons why* a referendum was held rather than allowing government and Parliament to decide the issue.

Examples of referendums in the UK

Having understood the reasons why referendums have been held in the UK, you can now look at Table 3, which shows the details of the key referendums that have taken place, together with their circumstances and results.

Table 3 Referendums in the UK

Year	Scope	Question	Circumstances	Outcome
1975	National	Should the UK remain a member of the European Community?	The newly elected Labour government was divided on the issue	A large 'yes' majority
1997	Scotland	Should Scotland have its own Parliament with significant powers?	An important constitutional change	A large 'yes' majority with a good turnout
1997	Scotland	Should a new Scottish Parliament have the power to vary income tax slightly from the level charged in the rest of Britain?	An issue affecting the level of tax	A large 'yes' majority with a good turnout
1997	Wales	Should Wales have an elected assembly with modest powers?	An important constitutional change	A narrow 'yes' majority with a low turnout
1998	Northern Ireland	Should the Belfast Agreement (also known as the Good Friday Agreement) be approved in order to bring peace and power sharing to Northern Ireland government?	An overwhelming need to secure the approval of both sides of the community after years of conflict	A large 'yes' majority with a high turnout
1998	London	Should London have an elected mayor and assembly?	A constitutional change with implications for taxation	A large 'yes' majority with a low turnout
2011	Wales	Should the Welsh Assembly have more powers?	A constitutional change with possible taxation implications	A large 'yes' majority with a low turnout
2011	National	Should AV (the alternative-vote electoral system) be adopted for Westminster elections?	The new coalition government was divided on the issue and it was an important constitutional change	A large 'no' vote on a low turnout

Why has the use of referendums increased since 1997?

There are a number of reasons why referendums are increasingly used or proposed. Among these are the following:

- Since 1997 there has been greater interest in constitutional reform. It is considered important that any such reform receives the direct consent of the people.
- Most of the constitutional reforms have been introduced by the Labour Party. Referendums are a way of entrenching reform, preventing possible future Conservative governments from reversing them without popular consent. This was especially true of devolution.
- It is generally believed that the electorate is now better informed about politics than ever before. This means that the electorate is better able to make informed judgements. The internet has helped in this regard.

Knowledge check 4

Identify four reasons why referendums have become increasingly popular in the UK. In each case, give an example.

- Referendums have proved to be an effective way of heading off political opposition. This was true of the 2010 referendum that rejected the AV voting system and prevented a split within the coalition government. The 1998 referendum on the Good Friday Agreement in Northern Ireland also sent a message to the militant terrorists on both sides of the sectarian divide, that the wider community wanted peace and reconciliation between republicans and unionists.

The case for and against the use of future referendums in the UK

More referendums may take place in the UK in future. Questions could include:

- whether Britain should adopt the use of the euro
- whether any further **sovereignty** (ultimate power) should be transferred to the European Union (EU)
- whether Scotland should become an independent state

Table 4 shows the arguments for and against the use of more such referendums. Additional arguments can be made by reference to the general evaluation of direct democracy shown above. Referendums are a key element of direct democracy.

Table 4 Arguments for and against the further use of referendums in the UK

For	Against
People are becoming more accustomed to being consulted on key issues	It may make worse the already low level of respect people have for representative institutions
It is easier to inform people about issues because of the internet and social media	If there are too many votes, 'voter fatigue' may set in. Turnouts will thus be low, and the results will be less legitimate
There is less public confidence in politicians than there used to be	The highly politically motivated tabloid press in Britain may reduce rational arguments to emotional appeals
There has been a general fall in traditional forms of participation in politics. Referendums will involve more people politically	Referendums may prove to be a kind of public opinion poll on the government rather than on the issue itself. This may have happened in 2010 when the 'no' vote on the introduction of the AV voting system was partly a judgement on the performance of the Liberal Democrats, who had sponsored the proposal

Examiner tip

Make sure you know at least four examples of important referendums held in the UK since 1975. Know why each one was held, what was the question and what was the outcome.

Other conceptions of democracy

The following conceptions of democracy are variations of representative democracy, as described above. There is considerable overlap between them. On the whole they suggest different emphases rather than different types of democracy.

Liberal democracy

Liberal democracy

A kind of democracy that conforms to liberal political principles, notably respect for rights and liberties, a strong constitutional framework, tolerance and the rule of law.

- **Liberal democracy** is a response to fears of the '**tyranny of the majority**', that is too much power in the hands of a dominant majority. To counteract this, a liberal democracy normally incorporates a Bill of Rights to protect the interests of individuals and minorities.

- Power is normally divided and separated in a liberal democracy. In other words, there are mechanisms for preventing too much power falling into too few hands. The so-called '**separation of powers**' distributes power between different branches of government.
- As well as separating powers there is a system of '**checks and balances**' in place. This means that the different branches of government — the legislature, the executive and the judiciary — have means by which they can control each other's power.
- There is a strong sense of '**constitutionalism**'. This means a strong constitution ensures the separation of powers, the system of checks and balances and the protection of individual and group rights.
- Liberal democracy cherishes the rights of the individual and of organisations. Thus there are strong safeguards for such freedom.
- Liberal democracy also implies a tolerant society, where diverse beliefs, groups and interests are allowed to flourish as long as they do not threaten the security of the state or the freedom of others.

A key example of a liberal democracy would be the USA.

Pluralist democracy

Pluralist democracies generally conform to the criteria of liberal democracy shown above. In addition, they have the following characteristics:
- There tends to be a large number of different political parties.
- There will also be a wide variety of political associations and pressure groups, which are tolerated and which may participate in political processes.
- Generally speaking, in a pluralist democracy, power is widely dispersed. This means that the people have a great deal of influence and power is not concentrated in a few hands.

A key example of a pluralist democracy would be Germany.

Parliamentary democracy

It is generally understood that this kind of parliamentary democracy is unique to the UK. To a large (though not total) extent, the UK conforms to the principles of liberal democracy, but it also has its own special character. Its characteristics are as follows:
- Parliament is sovereign and has ultimate political power.
- Laws will only be enforced if legitimised by the UK Parliament.
- Government is drawn from Parliament (all ministers must also be MPs or peers) and is part of Parliament.
- Parliament ensures the geographical representation of all parts of the UK.

The key example here is of course the UK.

Parliamentary democracy A kind of liberal democracy where a parliament is the central body and is the source of all political power.

Democracy in the UK

The nature and state of democracy in the UK can be viewed from three perspectives:
1 The nature of political institutions
2 The nature of political processes
3 The nature of political participation

After a brief look at forms of political participation in the UK, there follows an evaluation of democracy in the UK from each of these three perspectives.

Political participation in the UK

There are a number of ways in which people can and do participate in politics in the UK. These forms of political participation can include the following. The list is broadly organised according to the depth of the participation, starting with a minimum level. The early examples are shallow participation; the later ones are deeper and more extensive:

- making oneself informed about political issues, mainly through the media
- making one's views known in consultation processes, often though the internet
- voting regularly in elections or referendums
- making one's political views known through social media
- joining a political party
- joining a pressure group
- becoming active in a party or pressure group or through the media
- standing for office at local, regional or national level

Political participation
A reference to the fact that many citizens take part in some form of political activity. Participation can be minimal, for example by being informed and perhaps voting from time to time, or it can be deep, for example by seeking election to a public office and becoming a political leader.

Strengths (positive aspects) of UK democracy

Political institutions

- There is strong representation of individuals and constituencies by MPs.
- Parliament represents constituency, regional and national interests.
- There are free political parties and pressure groups.
- Government has a clear mandate to govern, against which it can be made accountable.
- The **rule of law** applies, ensuring equality under the law and that government does not act in an arbitrary manner but within legal constraints.
- The European Convention on Human Rights (ECHR) is binding on all bodies other than the UK Parliament.
- Significant powers have been decentralised, largely through the devolution process.
- The judiciary is politically independent.

Political processes

- Elections are free and are held regularly.
- Pressure groups have access to various levels of government.
- There is a free media and free access to independent information.
- Referendums are held to determine important constitutional issues.

Political participation

- All competent adults are permitted to participate in political processes.
- There is freedom of association, of thought and of belief.
- There is an increasing variety of pressure groups, often with large and rising memberships or numbers of supporters, including environmental groups such

as Greenpeace and Friends of the Earth, sectional groups such as Age UK, and campaign groups such as Liberty.
- Direct forms of political action on single issues are increasing, notably after 2010 on cuts in state service provision, university tuition fees, the privatisation of forests and NHS reform.

Criticisms (negative aspects) of UK democracy

Political institutions

- There remain some 'undemocratic' institutions, such as the unelected House of Lords and the monarchy.
- The (prerogative) powers of the prime minister are only conventional and not subject to law.
- The sovereignty of Parliament means that government is dominant when it controls Parliament and rights are at the mercy of a parliamentary majority.
- The European Convention on Human Rights and common law rights can be overturned by the UK Parliament, which remains sovereign.
- It is argued by many that too much power has been surrendered to the EU and this power is not accountable enough.

Political processes

- Elections are considered by many to be unfair and undemocratic. The first-past-the-post system distorts party representation.
- Parliament is relatively weak in its ability to call government to account, scrutinise legislation and represent different interests. This is the result of what many consider to be excessive government control.
- Smaller parties are under-represented.

Political participation

- Turnout at elections is low and has been falling in recent years. At general elections, turnout is typically 60–65%, whereas it was usually above 75% before the 1990s. Turnout among the young is especially low, as is turnout at devolved and local elections, often falling below 40%.
- Party membership has been falling, from a high point of over 2 million in all parties in the early 1980s to about 300,000 in 2010.
- There is widespread disillusionment with parties and politicians in general, resulting in a lack of identification with party policies.

Is the UK a liberal democracy?

This section considers the extent to which the UK can be said to be a true liberal democracy. In other words, how far does it conform to liberal democratic principles? Table 5 shows features which conform, those which do not and those where the picture is mixed.

Examiner tip

When evaluating the state of democracy in the UK, it is important to define first (though briefly) what is meant by 'democracy'. It is then possible to compare institutions and processes in the UK against that definition of democracy.

Table 5 To what extent does the UK conform to the principles of liberal democracy?

Features that conform	Features that do not conform	Mixed conformity
There are regular free elections	There is no codified and entrenched constitution	Elections by first-past-the-post are seen as unfair
Government is accountable to Parliament	The House of Lords is not elected	Rights are protected but can be set aside by the UK Parliament
Parties and pressure groups are tolerated	The prime minister has arbitrary (prerogative) powers	There is no separation of powers between the legislature and the executive (government)
There is a free media	There is an unelected head of state	
The rule of law applies		
There is an independent judiciary		

Knowledge check 5

Identify, using examples, three ways in which the UK conforms to the principles of liberal democracy and three ways in which it does not.

Improving democracy in the UK

It is often said in the modern age that there is a crisis in the UK democracy. A less dramatic judgement is that there is a 'democratic deficit'. This criticism has led to calls for various ways to improve the state of democracy.

The three tables below deal with possible remedies, based on the problems with institutions (Table 6), processes (Table 7) and participation (Table 8). In each case the proposals are critically examined.

Table 6 Proposals to improve democratic institutions in the UK and their assessment

Method	Assessment
Introducing an elected second chamber to replace the existing House of Lords	The new chamber may suffer the same problems as the House of Commons and not be independent of government
	The new chamber may have too much legitimacy and power and would challenge the authority of government
Introducing a codified constitution, especially to regulate the powers of the prime minister	A codified constitution may reduce the power of government excessively and reduce the flexibility of the political system
Making the European Convention on Human Rights binding on the UK Parliament	This may excessively reduce the power of Parliament, especially to maintain national security
Either taking the UK out of the EU altogether or reclaiming some of the powers already surrendered	The UK would lose the benefits of being an EU member
	The EU would probably not allow the UK to reclaim any of its national sovereignty
Granting further powers to devolved governments in Scotland, Wales and Northern Ireland, thus bringing democracy closer to the people	This may result in the break up of the UK
Making constituencies of equal size and so ensuring that votes are of more equal value	Population changes make this a difficult process. It may also lead to illogically organised constituencies

Table 7 Proposals to improve democratic processes in the UK and their assessment

Method	Assessment
Introducing a system of proportional representation for general elections to make the system more representative and to give smaller parties fair representation	Such a system would prevent any single party winning power. This would jeopardise strong, decisive government and eliminate the doctrine of the mandate because coalition governments do not have a clear mandate
	Coalition or minority governments would be more common and they are considered to be a weak form of government
	Proportional representation could introduce too many small parties, some of them extremists
Strengthening Parliament's ability to control government, for example by increasing its legislative powers	This might weaken government excessively and slow down the processes of government
Making the European Convention on Human Rights binding on the UK Parliament	This may excessively reduce the power of Parliament, especially to maintain national security
Introducing systems for **recalling** (in other words, 'unelecting') MPs who are unsatisfactory. This would make MPs more publicly accountable	This is a slow, cumbersome process which might fall into disuse because it is so difficult
	It may also be that recall attempts will be made for trivial reasons

Table 8 Proposals to improve democratic participation in the UK and their assessment

Method	Assessment
Granting votes to those aged 16 and over to bring young people into the political process and improve political education	Sixteen- and seventeen-years olds may have too little judgement to use their votes effectively
Introducing compulsory voting to force more people into the political process and to make the results of elections more legitimate	Compulsory voting could be seen as an infringement of individual liberty
	It would also force people with little or no political knowledge to vote. The results of elections would therefore be influenced by uninformed voters
Using more referendums to determine political issues and so widen participation	See Table 4 above for an assessment of the use of referendums
Using digital (internet-based) democracy as a means of consulting widely on issues	This may trivialise politics
	There is a danger with e-petitions that widespread fraud will be used
	This may also exclude a sizeable majority who do not use the internet
Using 'citizens' juries' and focus groups as a means of consulting representative samples of the population	Most of the population remain excluded, so participation is not widened
	There is no guarantee that such methods are truly representative

Knowledge check 6

Explain and assess briefly any three ways of increasing political participation in the UK.

Knowledge summary

- Knowledge and understanding of the nature of democracy in general
- Knowledge and understanding of different types of democracy
- Knowledge and understanding of the concept of legitimacy
- Knowledge and understanding of direct democracy and representative democracy, and explanation of the distinctions between them
- Analysis and evaluation of the relative merits of direct democracy and representative democracy
- Explanation of the nature of liberal democracy and evaluation of the extent to which the British political system conforms to its principles

- Knowledge and understanding of how democracy operates in the UK
- Explanation of the main problems with British democracy
- Knowledge and understanding of proposals to improve democracy in the UK
- Assessment and evaluation of proposals to improve democracy in the UK
- Knowledge and understanding of referendums held in the UK
- Evaluation of the proposed use of further referendums

Party policies and ideas
The nature of political parties

Political party A group of people who hold similar political beliefs and aspirations. They become a party when they seek power so that they can implement their aims or influence those who make decisions. In order to do this, they develop political programmes and campaign to gain members, followers and supporters.

Political parties form no official part of the UK Constitution yet the constitution could not currently operate without them. Political parties are crucial in ensuring the effective operation of today's representative democracy.

Features of parties

- Each party is a grouping of individuals who hold in common a particular ideology and set of principles or values.
- Each party is united by ideas and values and wishes to promote these and manage the country by them.
- Parties normally have a formal organisation with a leadership, active members and a mass membership.
- Parties have mechanisms for developing policy, selecting candidates for office and identifying leaders.

The general public tends to view politics in terms of the policies and general image of political parties. Individuals often identify with a party and see politics through the general philosophy of that party. Many people believe a particular party represents their interests better than any of the others. However, such close identification with a party has become less common in recent decades.

Key functions of political parties

- Political parties aggregate ideas; they put together a comprehensive and coherent set of policy options which are based on their political principles or ideas. They convert these policies into a workable political programme of action.

- They contest elections. In this process they provide ideas for the electorate, set out in a **manifesto**. A manifesto is a statement of policies and intentions.
- They select appropriate people to stand for election to local councils, to devolved assemblies in Scotland, Wales, Northern Ireland and Greater London, and to the UK Parliament.
- They provide the personnel of government. If a political party wins a general election, then the victorious party appoints its leading members to government.
- They provide representation and speak up for various sections of the community.
- They provide political education to the general public over which options the country should take.

The political spectrum

Political parties can be classified on a left to right political spectrum.

The political left

The '**left**' features the following typical ideas:
- **collectivism**, which is a belief that goals can be achieved by collective action as well as by the efforts of individuals. This includes the idea of the state as an essential and positive force in the lives of all
- a belief that the interests of the wider community are superior to the interests of individuals
- a belief in the universal distribution of benefits such as health, education, social insurance
- a positive view of human nature and a belief that people are essentially social animals, rather than self-seeking individuals
- the promotion of equality, fraternity and maximum freedom

Socialism is a clear example of left-wing beliefs.

The political right

The '**right**' features the following typical ideas:
- a firm belief in the importance of the individual and the provision of individual choice
- a belief that individuals have a flawed human nature and therefore need discipline
- a rejection of collectivism, with which right-wing politicians largely disagree
- a view that the role of the state in people's lives should be limited
- a view of human nature suggesting that individuals prefer to pursue their own goals and may see their own interests as more important than those of the wider community
- a belief that inequality and differences in living standards can be a positive force, creating incentives for individuals to improve themselves and not rely on the state
- a belief that the peace and security of the community is more important than the rights and freedoms of individuals

Traditional and 'New Right' conservatism are clear examples of right-wing beliefs.

Manifesto Before a general election, all political parties produce a manifesto. This is a statement of their intents and promises. Here they declare their political ideas and they set out their intended policies, which, if they are successful in the forthcoming election, they will implement. Success in the election is what triggers a manifesto of promises into positive governmental action.

Examiner tip
Be prepared to link both policy and ideas with the major political parties. Take note that these will change between elections, as parties continually develop new policy and ideas — you have to keep up to date here.

Left/right A way of characterising groups of political ideas. The left generally refers to those who have a tendency towards socialist or radically liberal ideas, while the right normally refers to a conservative or authoritarian state of political mind. The terms can be confusing and should be used with care.

Knowledge check 7

Identify and explain three of the key distinctions between the left and the right on the political spectrum.

Consensus and adversary politics

Building on from the opposite positions of left wing and right wing is the idea of consensus and adversary politics. Since 1945 the UK has been characterised as progressing through periods of consensus and adversary politics.

Consensus politics

Consensus politics is the position where there is widespread agreement over a good number of key areas of policy and ideas between the major parties competing for office. As a result there is little difference in how the country is governed, whichever party wins office. It also implies that policy makers will consult widely and secure wide agreement before putting policies into practice. It can also be described as a period when there are few **ideological** (that is, concerning fundamental beliefs) differences between parties and between factions within parties.

Consensus politics
A reference to political situations where there is widespread agreement between parties and groups on key political issues. It can also refer to a circumstance where there are few policy differences between major parties, or to a specific agreement between parties not to disagree on a particular issue.

Examples of consensus politics in the UK

The 'Butskellite' consensus (1945–79)

This consensus takes its name from two Chancellors of the Exchequer, R. A. Butler (Conservative) and Hugh Gaitskell (Labour). The Conservative Party came to accept the reforms of the 1945–51 Labour government. These included:

- a mixed economy , with some **nationalised** (state-run) industry and some private enterprises
- a belief in the importance of the welfare state
- acceptance of the power of organised labour through trade unions to balance the power of the employers
- a commitment in foreign policy to NATO and the close alliance with the USA

The post-Thatcher consensus (1994–2010)

The Labour Party, together with the Liberal Democrat Party (formed in 1988), slowly accepted the reforms of the Thatcher and Major governments of the 1980s and 1990s. These included:

- a commitment to the free market as often superior to state-run organisations
- a belief that most people prefer to be free to pursue their own individual goals, rather than pursuing them through collectivist organisations and the state
- a commitment to **privatisation** (the return of most large enterprises from the public to the private sector)
- a reduction in the importance and power of trade unions and the restoration of free labour markets
- a belief that welfare benefits can be a disincentive to work and enterprise and so should be reserved for those most in genuine need
- an acceptance that private sector enterprises should be able to compete with state-run organisations to provide state services

Adversary politics

Adversary politics can be said to exist when there is widespread and fundamental disagreement over the key policies and ideas of the main parties competing for governmental office. It also means there are deep ideological differences between parties and between factions within parties.

Example of adversary politics in the UK

The Labour/Conservative divide (1981–90)

While the Conservative Party, dominated by its leader Margaret Thatcher, moved to a right-wing position, Labour, under Michael Foot up to 1984 and then under Neil Kinnock, shifted to the left. Table 9 demonstrates the divide between the two.

Table 9 The adversary politics of the 1980s

'Thatcherite' conservative policies	Labour's left-wing response
The withdrawal of the state from control of most large-scale industries, and the selling off of such industries in a process known as privatisation	Opposing privatisation, together with policies to extend public ownership and state control (nationalisation) to more large enterprises
To reduce income tax in order to create greater incentives	To use relatively high income taxes to redistribute real income from rich to poor
Reducing welfare benefits as a means of creating more incentive to work and greater self-reliance	Extending welfare benefits to create more equality and to reduce poverty
To reduce drastically the power of trade unions to improve productivity and create free labour markets	Retaining powerful trade unions to protect the interests of workers against exploiting employers
Reducing state management of the economy, allowing free-market forces to operate. Concentrating on the control of inflation by controlling the amount of money in circulation (known as **monetarism**)	State management of the economy, including some centralised planning of production of key goods
Support for the European Community's free market (though not European political integration)	Britain to leave the European Community and to protect its own industries from competition
A strong defence policy, based on the nuclear deterrent, membership of NATO and a close alliance with the USA	An independent foreign policy with no nuclear deterrent

Adversary politics
A description of a circumstance where there are deep political differences between major parties and within parties. It can refer to a period when there are strong ideological conflicts.

Examiner tip
Do not confuse adversary politics with adversarial politics. They are significantly different and you will dramatically reduce your mark if you do not clarify the meaning of these terms. Adversarial politics refers to a style of politics where leaders appear to be antagonistic towards each other and demonstrate extreme levels of conflict. Prime Minister's Question Time in the UK is an example of adversarial politics.

Knowledge check 8
Look at the 2010 coalition agreement (you can find this on the internet) and make a note of three areas of consensus between the coalition partners and three agreements to differ.

The traditions and policies of the Labour Party

A brief history of Labour

1900	The trade union movement begins to put up candidates for office — effectively the founding of the party
1906	The party officially comes into existence
1906–45	The party is periodically in and out of government, either as a minority government or in coalition with other parties
1945–51	Labour gains power on its own and introduces a wide range of reforms in Britain based on socialism
1951–97	Labour is in and out of power
1997–2010	Labour is in power continuously

After the mid-1990s, the basic principles of the 'traditional' Labour Party became known as 'Old Labour', because so-called 'New Labour' had come into existence. The 'traditions' of Labour are set out in Table 10.

Traditional Labour

Table 10 Labour Party traditions

Ideas and principles	Examples of ideas and principles reflected in practical policies
Equality The idea that people are essentially of equal worth and that there should be no unjustified privileges or inequality in society. People are also entitled to equal rights	Artificial privileges should be removed or reduced Taxation and welfare benefits should be used to reduce differences in real incomes Wealth should not give anyone unjustified access to power
Collectivism and universalism A belief that most people prefer to achieve their goals collectively, rather than individually. Humankind is seen as a social animal, balancing own individual interests against those of the wider community. Furthermore, the collective provision of welfare should apply to all equally and universally	There should be a welfare state whereby such goods as healthcare, education, subsidised housing, social insurance, pensions and social care should be paid for out of general taxation and all should be equally entitled to their benefits Local government services are a vital aspect of collectivism Workers are best protected by unions rather than through laws protecting individuals

Ideas and principles	Examples of ideas and principles reflected in practical policies
Control of capitalism Capitalism can be tolerated but only if the exploitation of workers and consumers can be controlled, and if private enterprise serves the interests of the whole community	Key industries, including those providing infrastructure, energy and utilities, plus any natural monopolies, should be brought under public ownership and state control (nationalisation) Strong trade unions to defend the interests of workers Control over monopoly power
Social justice A belief and aspiration that all in society should have equal opportunities, should have access to a decent standard of living and should be able to improve their circumstances through their own merit	Provide education and other welfare benefits to widen personal opportunity The welfare state to guarantee living standards Strong laws to guarantee equal rights and to outlaw discrimination
Class and society Labour Party tradition argues that there is a fundamental division in society between classes, mainly the middle and working classes. The differences between classes need to be reconciled	The standard of living of the working class to be subsidised through progressive taxation and welfare provisions Strong trade unions represent the interests of the working class Firm economic management to control unemployment Controls over capitalism to reduce its exploitation of the working class Nationalisation to give the working class a greater stake in the economy.

New Labour

The term 'New Labour' refers to a complete change in the philosophy and policies of the Labour Party in the mid-1990s. Breaking away from 'Old' Labour ideas, as shown in Table 10, the party was transformed under the leadership of John Smith (1992–94) and Tony Blair (1994–2007). To some extent the party adopted the so-called 'post-Thatcher consensus' (see p. 20).

New Labour also followed a set of ideas known as the '**third way**', an idea developed by sociologist Anthony Giddens in the early 1990s. The third way refers to a centre path steered between the old Labour tradition, which was partly socialist in essence, and the New Right policies (see pp. 27–28) of the Conservative Party in the 1980s.

The ideas and policies of New Labour are set out in Table 11.

Table 11 New Labour and the 'third way'

Ideas and principles	Examples of ideas and principles reflected in practical policies
Individualism The old collectivist ideas of Labour were replaced by a greater emphasis on individualism, the ability of the individual to realise his or her own goals and aspirations	Lower personal taxation, introduced by the Conservatives, to be retained to encourage work and enterprise Home ownership to be encouraged and supported Small businesses to be encouraged and supported A stress on education, including the expansion of higher education, to maximise the ability of individuals to widen their opportunities and to be socially mobile, to improve their living standards and status
The free market Labour accepted that free-market capitalism was the best form of wealth creator. The state should only take control of enterprises when they cannot be made to act in the public interest	No return to nationalisation of industries and some further privatisation to take place when justified Reduced corporate taxes to encourage enterprise, innovation and investment Private sector enterprises to be able to compete with public sector organisations in such areas as school and hospital building, local government services, prisons, road maintenance Continued support for weak trade unions to ensure free labour markets
The welfare state New Labour fully supported the welfare state and increased state spending in that area. However, welfare benefits were to be used as an incentive, rather than a disincentive, to work and self-reliance. Welfare to be targeted to those in most need rather than being universally available	Increased spending on health and education Welfare benefits to be reformed; to be targeted on those in most need and withheld from those who do not seek work Improved efficiency by allowing the private sector to compete to provide services for the welfare state
Social justice New Labour shared many of the beliefs and ideas of traditional Labour	Provide education and other welfare benefits to widen personal opportunity. Special stress on higher education and pre-school education The welfare state to guarantee living standards Strong laws to guarantee equal rights and to outlaw discrimination The minimum wage to eliminate unacceptably low wages A general attack on child poverty through the welfare and education systems The tax credit system to guarantee minimum standards of living
Communitarianism New Labour replaced the old Labour belief in the class system with an idea known as 'communitarianism'. This is a belief that, in a world of free-market capitalism and individualism, all still have a responsibility to care for the community collectively	A caring attitude to the environment, with strong green policies An emphasis on schools, local welfare services and strong social services State support for local voluntary associations
Ethical foreign policy A belief that Britain has a responsibility for poorer parts of the world and that caring for the developing world is in Britain's self-interest	Increasing foreign aid Campaigning to cancel 'third world' debt Campaigning for more free-market policies in world trade Intervening abroad where democracy and human rights are threatened

Key distinctions and similarities between traditional ('Old') and 'New' Labour

The main distinctions, summarised, include the following:

- New Labour stresses individualism, whereas Old Labour stresses collectivism.
- Old Labour sought to modify and regulate capitalism, creating a mixed economy of both public and private sector. New Labour accepts free-market capitalism and encourages it.
- Old Labour saw the state as a key means by which society can be improved. New Labour sees the role of the state as merely enabling individuals to prosper.
- Old Labour saw society in terms of class conflict, whereas New Labour thinks class is insignificant and that individual interests are more important than class interests.
- Old Labour sought to promote economic and social equality, whereas New Labour sees inequality as natural and something that can be tolerated as long as there is equality of opportunity and opportunities are enhanced.

The main similarities are summarised below. Both Old and New Labour believe:

- in fundamental social justice — that excessive inequality in society is unacceptable
- that the welfare state is a key element in creating and maintaining social justice
- that there should be widespread equality of opportunity
- that there should be equal rights and no artificial discrimination against any sections of society
- that, in a capitalist society, private enterprises need to be regulated to ensure they do not act against the public interest

The Labour Party under Ed Miliband (since 2010)

Following the defeat of the Labour government in the 2010 general election, Gordon Brown was replaced as leader by Ed Miliband. Both Brown and Miliband have their roots in New Labour and there will be few major departures in policy. It is too early, in 2011, to see in which direction Labour will be moving. The following tendencies, however, can be discerned:

- Labour will continue to emphasise education as the main driver of social justice and social mobility.
- There are likely to be more state interventions in certain key sectors of the economy. This may involve new company tax policies and public investment in industry — in other words, more state intervention than under New Labour. The industries concerned might include green technology, information technology, bio research and technology, and electronics.
- There is likely to be greater stress on environmental protection.
- The party will be in favour of more active state intervention to promote more economic growth in general.

Factions (tendencies) in the Labour Party

Factionalism in the Labour Party is not well defined and so its factions are better described as 'tendencies'. The party remains largely united around policies developed

Examiner tip

Beware of describing the Labour Party as ever being 'socialist' in nature. Many of its members used to describe themselves as socialist, as have some of their enemies, but this can be misleading. Labour has always been only a mildly socialist party.

Factionalism Applied to political parties, this term refers to the groupings and tendencies within a political party. These groups agree with the central beliefs of the party but place a greater emphasis on some particular ideas. It is common for certain factions to be dominant at times in a political party's historical evolution. Some factions may break away and leave the party. Several moderate members of the Labour Party, for example, left the party in the 1980s and went to form the SDP.

Knowledge check 9

Briefly explain any four ways in which New Labour differs from traditional Labour.

under Tony Blair and Gordon Brown. However, there are some tendencies which can be discerned. The three main ones are these:

- **New Labour traditionalists** — those who support the principles of the 'third way', developed in the 1990s. Harriet Harman MP, David Miliband MP and Ed Balls MP are important examples
- **The left** — those who still support many traditional Labour policies, including radical redistribution of income, the restoration of trade union power and the return of some major industries to state control
- **The right and Blue Labour** — this group, sometimes referred to as 'Blue Labour', support a number of Conservative Party policies including the 'big society', opposition to high levels of immigration and more local control over health and education. Leading figures are Maurice (Lord) Stearman and Marc Stears

The traditions and policies of the Conservative Party

A brief history of the Conservative Party

There is no single point in time when the Conservative Party came into existence. It is generally accepted, however, that the Conservative Party in a modern sense came into existence in the 1830s under the leadership of Robert Peel. Since then the party has gradually developed a more formal structure and membership. For most of the nineteenth century and the early part of the twentieth, the Conservative Party was largely engaged in resisting the reforms proposed by the Whigs and later the Liberals. In other words, it stood for tradition and stability (conservatism). For most of the twentieth century the party also fought against the growing force of socialism. In this conflict it became a strong supporter of free-market capitalism and individualism. In 1975 Margaret Thatcher became leader of the party. Between then and her downfall in 1990, Thatcher transformed the party, modelling it on her own political philosophy known as 'Thatcherism', 'neo-liberalism' and 'neo-conservatism'.

Conservatism A term that can simply mean a state of mind that is resistant to change and innovation. In politics, it refers to a more specific political movement that opposed the radical elements of socialism and liberalism since the nineteenth century. Despite variations, most Conservatives support tradition, the maintenance of law and order, free markets and the pursuit of individualism.

Traditional conservatism

Table 12 shows the beliefs and policies of the 'traditional' Conservative Party, that is, those ideas that pre-date Thatcher.

Table 12 Traditional conservative beliefs

Ideas and principles	Examples of ideas and principles reflected in practical policies
Order Traditional conservatives believe that order in society is a strong human need. Without good order, progress cannot be achieved	Strong authoritarian policies on law and order Taking a hard line against organised protest in society A general belief in strong government

Ideas and principles	Examples of ideas and principles reflected in practical policies
Organic society This is a twofold philosophy. First, it suggests that society is like a living organism and should be allowed to develop naturally, without artificial intervention. Second, it is a view that all the sections of society depend on each other and are part of a single whole. We are not merely free individuals	Parties and governments should not seek to impose their own beliefs upon society Policies should be aimed at maintaining a strong, united society
Fear of diversity The belief in an organic society leads to a fear of too much social and cultural diversity that might threaten social unity	Opposition to multiculturalism Resistance to high levels of immigration Intolerance towards 'unconventional lifestyles'
Support for tradition Conservatives believe that traditions are important in maintaining unity and continuity with the past. They provide a means by which a society can unite around common institutions and values. Traditions refer to both institutions and values	Opposition to reforms that threaten traditional institutions, such as electoral reform, reform of the House of Lords, a changed role for the monarchy or movement towards a codified constitution Strong support for traditional values, largely surrounding the traditional family and traditional morality. As far as possible the state should support these values through its policies
Support for private property and accumulated wealth Conservatives see the ownership of property and wealth as being important in two main ways. First, property and wealth are an expression of a family's individualism and their aspirations. Second, property and wealth create a sense of responsibility. Those who enjoy them have a greater sense of responsibility. Furthermore, those who enjoy wealth and status have a responsibility to help those less fortunate. This last doctrine is known as *noblesse oblige*	Taxes on property and wealth should be held down and possibly eliminated The rights of property owners should be protected, notably through strong policies on law and order and privacy laws Conservatives have supported the idea that the wealthy should support the underprivileged, but largely through the voluntary sector rather than through high taxation
Pragmatism It is a principle of conservatism that each problem in government should be dealt with on its own merits and not according to any fixed doctrines or ideology. Thus Conservatives have opposed socialism and liberalism as fixed doctrines	Policies to be judged on their merits. Those which seem to favour the public good should be retained and those which do not, rejected, no matter whether they come from left- or right-wing ideas In foreign policy, Britain's national interest should always be pursued

Examiner tip

Make sure you understand the differences between terms that sound similar — for example 'New Right', neo-liberalism and neo-conservatism. Note also that neo-liberalism is considered to be a 'right-wing' philosophy even though it proposes extreme economic freedom. Note also that neo-conservatives do not always agree with traditional conservatives.

New Right or 'Thatcherite' conservatism

Under the leadership of Margaret Thatcher (1975–90), the Conservative Party changed its political position. She transformed the party completely, especially after 1982. Table 13 sets out the main ideas and principles of the New Right, together with the practical policies which arose from them.

Table 13 The New Right under Margaret Thatcher

Ideas and principles	Examples of ideas and principles reflected in practical policies
The free market and neo-liberalism Margaret Thatcher and her leadership group were 'neo-liberals'. They believed that, wherever possible, all markets should be free from intervention or interference by government, by trade unions or by large, powerful corporations. The solution to virtually all economic problems lay in free markets correcting themselves automatically. This meant free markets for products, finance and in the supply of labour	Most large, nationalised (publicly owned and state-run) industries were sold off into private hands. These included gas, electricity and water, telecommunications, steel, coal and railways (railways were privatised very late, in 1996) Some industries were made open to competition and monopolies were broken up. These included the professions (law, opticians etc.). The financial markets were made more open and competitive, banks were allowed to compete with building societies State-run services were opened up to competition between the state itself and private companies
Anti-unionism The New Right believed that powerful trade unions were a barrier to economic progress. They prevented labour markets being flexible, forced wages up too high and prevented technological progress in many industries	The legal powers of trade unions were severely reduced Unions were forced to make themselves more internally democratic to break up unaccountable leadership groups The ability of unions to take industrial action to further their aims was reduced
Low direct taxation New Right conservatives saw direct taxes on individuals and private companies as a disincentive to work and enterprise	Income tax rates were reduced, especially at higher earning levels. The revenue was made up by higher indirect taxes such as VAT Taxes on private company profits were reduced
State disengagement from economic management As neo-liberals, these conservatives believed that economic problems would solve themselves in the medium term, as long as governments resisted the temptation to try to manage the economy. The only justifiable intervention was in controlling the total amount of money in circulation (the money supply) to prevent inflation. This policy was known as monetarism	Government did not intervene when there were economic slumps in the early 1980s and 1990s Government controlled the money supply tightly
Dependency culture Thatcherite conservatives saw excessively high levels of welfare benefits as a disincentive to work, enterprise and self-reliance. This created a 'dependency culture' where people became used to relying on state support	Many welfare benefits were reduced or eliminated Benefits were targeted on those in most need, and who were unable to be self-reliant through no fault of their own
Neo-conservatism Recognising that a much freer society could create the danger of disorder and moral decline, the New Right adopted American neo-conservative ideals. These included a strong position on law and order and attempts to maintain traditional, Christian morality. Excessive cultural diversity was discouraged	Strong policing policies, including greater powers to control demonstrations and public disorder Longer, more severe sentences for criminals Support for the institution of traditional marriage
Property Like traditional conservatives, the New Right emphasised the importance of home ownership	Tenants in local authority housing were given the right to buy their homes at discounted prices and mortgage rates The markets supplying mortgages were opened up to greater competition and it was made easier for families to obtain mortgages and credit generally

Key distinctions and similarities between traditional and New Right conservatism

The main distinctions, summarised, include the following:
- Traditional conservatives see society as organic, whereas the New Right sees society as no more than a collection of individuals. Margaret Thatcher famously stated, 'there is no such thing as society'.
- Traditional conservatives support free markets but take a pragmatic view of economic management, believing that there are times when state intervention is needed. The New Right is ideologically opposed to state intervention.
- Traditional conservatives have favoured a mixed economy, with some key industries remaining under state control. The New Right has been determined to virtually eliminate state control of industry and commerce.
- Traditional conservatives are more supportive of the welfare state than the New Right.
- While traditional conservatives take a pragmatic view of policies generally, judging each case on its merits, the New Right is more ideological and tends to govern on the basis of its fixed ideas.

The main similarities, summarised, include the following:
- Both strands of conservatism take an authoritarian view of law and order issues.
- Both support traditional Christian, family and 'British' values.
- Both have an instinct for free markets and low taxation, although the New Right is more dogmatic about these principles, while traditional conservatives are more pragmatic.
- Both see private property ownership as a key element leading to social responsibility and order.
- Both movements are nationalist in outlook and are determined to pursue British national interests.

Knowledge check 10

Explain briefly any four ways in which Thatcherite or New Right conservatism differs from traditional conservatism.

The Conservative Party under David Cameron (since 2005)

The Conservative Party under Cameron can be seen as a combination of neo-liberalism, traditional conservatism and liberalism. It has also been influenced by the need to retain a consensus between it and its Liberal Democrat partners in coalition. Its main features are as follows.

Traditional conservative elements
- Cameron and his supporters tend to adopt a pragmatic approach to politics.
- They are committed to traditional institutions and values.
- They are committed to protecting the rights and interests of property owners.
- They believe the wealthy do have a responsibility to help to improve the conditions of the disadvantaged.

New Right elements

- The party is still committed to the free market and maximising economic competition.
- It seeks to keep direct taxes as low as possible.
- It is committed to financial responsibility, and preventing the state from overspending and interfering in economic activity.
- It hopes to promote more competition and private sector involvement in the provision of services to the welfare state.
- It seeks to target welfare benefits on those in most need and to attack benefits which are seen as a disincentive to work.

Liberal elements

- The party under Cameron accepts diversity in society and promotes tolerance of different groups and cultures.
- It is seeking to strengthen the protection of individual rights and liberties.
- It accepts the need to reduce inequality in society.
- The 'big society' idea encourages voluntary community action and local democracy.
- There is cautious interest in constitutional reforms.
- The Conservative Party places more emphasis on environmental protection than ever before.

Factions within the Conservative Party

Table 14 shows the three main factions within the Conservative Party in 2011. In each case the main ideals of the group are shown, together with some leading members.

Table 14 Conservative Party factions

Faction	Ideals	Leading Members
Conservative Way Forward	Embraces the policies of Margaret Thatcher from the 1980s, including neo-liberalism and neo-conservatism	Christopher Chope MP Lord Tebbitt Don Porter
Tory Reform Group	They see themselves as traditional 'one-nation' conservatives. They are liberal in their philosophy, supporting social justice, individual liberty and moderate law and order policies	Kenneth Clarke MP Damian Green MP Alistair Burt MP
Cameronian conservatives	Supporters of David Cameron's philosophy: a combination of neo-liberalism, orthodox liberalism, welfare reformers and big society advocates	David Cameron MP George Osborne MP Andrew Lansley MP

The traditions and policies of the Liberal Democrat Party

A brief history of the Liberal Democrat Party

The Liberal Democrat Party came into existence in 1988. It was the fusion of the Liberal Party, which had been in existence since the later nineteenth century and was in long-term decline, and the Social Democratic Party (SDP). The SDP was an offshoot from the Labour Party in 1981. It contained moderate social democrats who opposed the shift to the left of the Labour Party in the early 1980s. The ideals of the Liberal Democrat Party (the Lib Dems) are therefore a combination of liberalism and social democracy (an extremely mild form of socialism).

Ideas and policies of the Lib Dems

Table 15 shows the main influences on the Liberal Democrat Party from liberalism and from social democracy. Table 16 shows how these ideas have been combined in the Liberal Democrat Party and gives examples of policies that reflect those ideas.

Liberalism A philosophy dating back to the eighteenth century. It has individual liberty at the centre of its belief system. It also refers to a collection of ideas including tolerance, constitutionalism, social justice and equality of opportunity.

Table 15 Influences on the Liberal Democrat Party

Liberal ideas	Social democratic ideas
The vital importance of individual liberties and rights	The welfare state must play a key role in society
Equal rights for individuals and groups	Social justice should be promoted by the state by redistributing income from rich to poor
The destruction of artificial privileges	Equality of opportunity to increase both social justice and the widening of opportunities
Tolerance of differing beliefs, movements and cultures	A mixed economy with some strategic economic activities under state control
Constitutionalism — a belief that there needs to be strict legal rules to determine the operation of government and politics	The rights of workers under free-market capitalism to be protected
	Strong defence of the interests of consumers
Limited government to prevent the concentration of power in the state	Acceptance that private enterprise is the most effective way of creating wealth
The maximisation of democracy and the dispersal of power as widely as possible	An open economy, with free competition in world markets

Table 16 Liberal Democrat beliefs

Ideas and principles	Examples of ideas and principles reflected in practical policies
Liberalism	Strong laws to protect rights and liberties
	Tolerance enshrined in anti-discrimination laws
	Equal rights legislation
Constitutionalism	Support for the introduction of a codified, entrenched constitution controlling governmental power and dispersing power
	Constitutional reform proposals to modernise, liberalise, democratise and decentralise government and politics

Ideas and principles	Examples of ideas and principles reflected in practical policies
Social justice	Taxation policies to redistribute real income from rich to poor. Higher taxes on the very rich
	Policies in education and employment to widen opportunity and increase social mobility
Liberal position on law and order	Policies that recognise that crime is in large part caused by poor social conditions
	Sentencing to take account of the social causes of crime and directed at rehabilitation rather than punishment
Welfarism	Strong support for the welfare state
	Welfare benefits to reduce poverty, support the disadvantaged and promote the value of work
	Education seen as the key driver for social justice
European Union	The EU is a positive force and should be supported and integration encouraged
	Britain should become more integrated in the EU
	Britain should adopt the euro as soon as feasible
Environmentalism	Ambitious plans for control over climate change
	Policies to transfer the UK to renewable energy sources as soon as possible
Localism	Local taxation to be reformed to make it 'fairer'
	Strengthening local government in comparison to central government
	Improving local democracy

The Orange Book group

There is only one major group of dissidents within the Liberal Democrat Party. It is named after the 'Orange Book', a collection of policy ideas published in 2004. Leading contributors to the Orange Book included David Laws MP and Chris Huhne MP, both members of the original 2010 coalition cabinet. Three of this group's main variations from conventional Liberal Democrat ideas are as follows:

- a belief in free markets and opposition to excessive state intervention in the economy and society generally
- a sceptical attitude to the effectiveness of the EU and scepticism concerning many of its policies including the Common Agricultural Policy (CAP)
- an emphasis on the need for more powerful local government to counterbalance the power of the central state

A summary of political difference and consensus

The following list of policy areas, grouped according to level of agreement, highlights some key examples of points of difference and consensus between the three main parties in the UK.

Consensus issues

- There needs to be some further constitutional reform, notably of the House of Lords.
- There needs to be a dramatic improvement in the use of renewable resources and in the rate of reduction of harmful emissions (though Liberal Democrats oppose the extension of nuclear energy).
- British foreign policy should remain under the umbrella of NATO.
- All parties now believe that free-market capitalism is the best form of wealth creation.
- There is general agreement that the welfare state should be protected.

Partial consensus

- Labour and the Conservatives tend to follow American foreign policy. The Liberal Democrats prefer an independent foreign policy.
- Liberal Democrats are enthusiastic about European integration. Labour is cautiously pro the EU, but waits for the right time to join the euro system. Conservatives are Eurosceptics and oppose Britain ever adopting the euro.
- The three parties agree that immigration needs to be controlled, but the Conservatives seek to control it more than others.
- While all parties wish to see some private sector involvement in welfare provision, the Conservatives are most enthusiastic about private sector involvement and more competition.

Main issues in conflict

- There are important differences over law and order policy. Liberal Democrats support liberal policies, dealing with the causes of crime rather than mere punishment; Conservatives take a hard line on crime; while Labour is somewhere between the two.
- The three parties differ a good deal about how much taxation should be used to redistribute real income from rich to poor.
- The Conservatives support radical measures to reduce the level of government debt. Labour and the Liberal Democrats disagree, favouring a more gradual approach to avoid a recession.
- There is much conflict over how higher education is to be funded. Conservatives support the use of high tuition fees, Liberal Democrats oppose tuition fees (though this policy was abandoned as part of the coalition agreement), while Labour prefers a mix of tuition fees and state provision from taxpayers' money.

Examiner tip

Points of consensus and conflict in politics are constantly shifting. Make sure you keep up to date with new developments.

Knowledge summary

- Knowledge and understanding of the key characteristics of political parties in the UK
- Knowledge and understanding of the terms left wing and right wing and the scope of the political spectrum
- Knowledge and explanation of the functions of political parties in a representative democracy
- Full appreciation of the terms consensus and adversary politics and how they differ, with accurate examples of each
- Full appreciation of the ideological core principles of socialism and how it applies to the Labour Party
- Full appreciation of the ideological core principles of conservatism and how it applies to the Conservative Party
- Full appreciation of the ideological core principles of liberalism and how it applies to the Liberal Democrat Party
- Understanding and analysis of the groups and factions that exist within the major political parties

Election An occasion when voters are given the opportunity to choose a representative. Elections in the UK occur at local, regional, national and European levels.

Examiner tip

It is unlikely you will need to explain more than three or four functions of elections, so ensure you know four of the most important. These should include electing representatives, granting a mandate to government, holding the outgoing government to account and choosing between competing sets of policies and leaders.

Mandate A principle that, when a government is elected, it is considered to have the authority to carry out the commitments made in its election manifesto.

Elections

Elections are a key feature of the UK's representative democracy, used at various levels of government. Free and fair elections are a hallmark of democracy. Several different voting systems now exist in the UK, but there are basic functions common to all elections.

Functions of elections

- Elections allow a geographical area to have a representative in a collective assembly to speak on behalf of those living in the area.
- Elections offer representation for political parties.
- Elections provide a means whereby the population selects a government. In the UK, the government is not directly elected but is obtained indirectly though elections to Parliament. In Parliament the party (or parties) which can secure enough seats form the government.
- Elections are a mechanism of legitimacy. They confer the authority to act on others' behalf. At a constituency level, this is conferring the right of an MP to act on behalf of the area; at a national level, a government claims legitimacy to act and manage the country.
- An election gives a mandate to the government of a locality, a region or the whole country. This means it gives legitimacy to the government's manifesto, or list of intended policies.
- Elections are mechanisms of accountability. They hold individual MPs in constituencies to account for their role as an area representative and they hold the government to account for its management of the country.
- Elections are mechanisms of choice. Not only do people choose their representatives and government, voting in an election is the expression of policy preferences, as citizens vote for certain policies and options.
- Elections have an educative function. In the competitive nature of campaigning for votes, citizens become informed of the major issues concerning the state.

Elections and democracy

Table 17 is an evaluation of elections, demonstrating ways in which they enhance democracy and how they can be seen as undemocratic.

Table 17 Do elections promote democracy in the UK?

Yes	No
Democracy is about choice; elections provide that choice	The choice on offer is limited to the mainstream parties, all offering similar polices: that is not a real choice
Democracy is about all citizens having an equal input and say in choosing representatives. In elections we all have one vote = one value	Not all citizens' votes are equal. Those in marginal seats for Westminster elections can be more valuable than those in safe seats. Votes are of unequal value
Elections are the best mechanism for democracy, given the impractical nature of direct democracy in the UK with over 45 million voters	Elections are *not* the best mechanism for democracy; more direct methods of democracy should replace them, such as referendums and e-democracy
Elections are free for all to contest and stand in. All that is required is a deposit, which is returned on collection of a certain minimum number of votes	In reality only those who are supported by an organised and widely recognised major political party stand a reasonable chance of success. Individuals and groups with poor funding stand little chance of winning elections
Many, though not all, see the electoral system used to elect the UK Parliament as fair, as it ensures that the individual with the most votes in each area wins the election	The Westminster electoral system is flawed. Only one-third of MPs gain 50% of the vote in their constituencies and no government for over 80 years has ever got 50% of the national vote
As there is freedom of expression, elections enhance democracy by educating and informing the public	Governments and politicians lack democratic legitimacy through elections if they are put in place by less than 30% of the population
A significant number of elections are on offer in the UK, providing choice and opportunity to influence the agenda	The only real election which counts is the one for MPs at Westminster, held on average every 4 to 5 years. It could be said that elections are too far apart to make government truly accountable

Knowledge check 12

How did the coalition government, formed in 2010, challenge the doctrines of manifesto and mandate?

Types of election held in the UK

There is a wide variety of elections held in the UK. They take place at European, national, regional and local levels. A range of different types of representative are chosen, and a variety of electoral systems are used. This variety is set out in Table 18.

Table 18 Outline of elections held in the UK

Where	Representative	Voting system
Westminster (London)	Members of Parliament (MPs)	Simple plurality (first-past-the-post)
European Union (Brussels/ Strasbourg)	Members of the European Parliament (MEPs)	Closed party list

Where	Representative	Voting system
Devolved Parliament Scotland (Edinburgh)	Members of the Scottish Parliament (MSPs)	Additional member system
Welsh Assembly (Cardiff)	Assembly Members (AMs)	Additional member system
Northern Irish Assembly (Stormont, Belfast)	Member of the Legislative Assembly	Single transferable vote
London	Mayor of London	Supplementary vote
Greater London Authority	Assembly Members	Additional member system
Local government, England and Wales	Local and county councillors	Simple plurality (first-past-the-post)
Local government, Scotland	Local and county councillors	Single transferable vote

Electoral or voting systems

There are a number of different electoral systems operating in the UK, depending on who is being elected. Each one is described below.

Britain's main electoral system (first-past-the-post)

The main electoral system in the UK, known as first-past-the post, is a plurality system. It is used for elections to the UK Parliament, and to English and Welsh local government. It is also used in the USA and India.

Operation

A simple plurality system means that the winner is the candidate who gains the most votes. The winning margin need only be one vote; quite often it is less than 50% of the votes cast.

Voters simply put an 'X' in the box, indicating their choice. There is no order of preference.

The UK is divided up into 650 constituencies. These are single-member constituencies, that is, only one MP is returned per constituency.

The 'winning post' in a constituency is determined after all the votes have been counted; whoever gets the highest number of votes wins the seat. The winning margin could be as small as one and or as huge as over 20 thousand.

The winning post required to form a government from the results of these constituency elections is, however, fixed. With a total of 650 seats, if one party gains 326 MPs this gives it a majority of two over all others. In May 2010, no party reached this total.

Apart from a few exceptions, all adults over 18 years of age and who are UK citizens are allowed to vote. Exceptions include most prisoners (this has become a controversial issue, with the European Court of Human Rights ordering Britain to allow them to vote in a 2010 judgement), and those certified with serious mental illness.

Impacts

The first-past-the-post system tends to produce a clear winner at general elections. In other words, one party usually wins over 50% of the seats in the House of Commons. This means that the winning party can form a government on its own and can rely on a parliamentary majority.

In February 1974 and May 2010, the system did not produce such a clear winner. In 1974, a minority Labour government was formed. In 2010, a Conservative–Liberal Democrat coalition was formed.

The system favours those parties whose electoral support is geographically concentrated. This applies mostly to Labour, and to a lesser extent to the Conservatives and nationalist parties. This is because parties whose support is dispersed tend to be unable to win the necessary 35%-plus of the votes in most constituencies. The Liberal Democrats and small parties such as the Green Party, the BNP and UKIP suffer most markedly.

Most MPs are elected with less than an **absolute majority** (over 50%) of votes in their own constituency; in other words, more people voted against them than for them.

Many votes are 'wasted' — either they are cast for candidates with no hope of winning or they are in 'safe' seats where the result is inevitable because one party is dominant.

The winning party is elected with less than a majority of the popular vote (the votes for the party in all constituencies added up). Labour 'won' in 2005 with just 35% of the popular vote. However, the 2010 coalition government could claim to have won a majority of votes, though the Conservatives won only 36% of the popular vote.

Some voters, who recognise that the candidate they support is unlikely to win, vote 'tactically' — that is, they do not vote for their favoured candidate, but for their second choice, who does have a chance of winning. In other words, voters may vote to 'keep out' a candidate they dislike, rather than vote for their favourite candidate.

The advantages and disadvantages of the first-past-the-post system are summarised in Table 19.

Table 19 A brief assessment of the first-past-the-post electoral system

Advantages	Disadvantages
It is easy to understand and operate	Most MPs do not have an absolute majority of support
It usually delivers a strong government by a single party (though 2010 weakened this claim)	Governments are normally elected without an absolute majority of the popular vote
There is a strong link between the voters and the constituency MP	It distorts the result in that the proportion of seats won by each party does not match the proportion of votes each party wins
It is well established and provides continuity	It discriminates against small parties
	A large number of votes are wasted
	It encourages voters to vote tactically rather than for their first choice

Knowledge check 13

Briefly explain three ways in which first-past-the-post is an effective electoral system, and three ways in which it is not.

Majoritarian representation This term relates to the *manner* in which votes are turned into seats. Majoritarian *systems* such as AV and SV aim to procure this. Majoritarian representation is also a product of the simple plurality system ('first-past-the-post'); as this has a strong tendency to over-reward the winning party, it is sometimes referred to as the 'winner's bonus'.

Proportional representation The concept whereby votes are converted into a corresponding percentage of seats. Hence, on a national scale, if a party obtains 30% of the vote then it would be awarded 30% of the seats in Parliament. It is at times referred to as 'fair voting'. There are numerous systems of achieving proportional representation.

Other electoral systems

Other electoral systems have been introduced in the UK for a number of reasons:
- Some were introduced into devolved systems. In Scotland and Wales it was felt undesirable if one party was able to dominate, so the simple first-past-the-post was replaced by the proportional additional member system.
- Similarly, in Northern Ireland, the highly proportional single transferable vote (STV) was used to ensure that all significant parties could share power.
- The regional list system for the European Parliament was essential to fall into line with the rest of Europe.
- The supplementary vote is the normal way of electing a single representative, hence its use to elect mayors.

These other voting systems fall into two categories, as detailed below.

Majority or majoritarian systems

Majority or majoritarian systems are those that ensure that the winning candidate or party has at least a 50% majority of first- and subsequent-choice votes. There are two main examples:
- the supplementary vote (SV), used to elect the London mayor
- the alternative vote (AV), a system not used in the UK after it was rejected in a referendum in 2011. (Technically, it is used for by-elections in Scottish and Northern Ireland local government, but this need not concern students.)

Majoritarian representation occurs when a party gets over 50% of the seats and can form a majority in the legislature.

Proportional representation

Voting systems that use **proportional representation** seek to ensure that the proportion of seats won by each party is approximately in proportion to the votes cast for each. The main examples are:
- single transferable vote (STV), used for elections in Northern Ireland and for local government in Scotland
- additional member system, used to elect the Scottish Parliament, the Welsh Assembly and the Greater London Assembly
- regional list system (closed), used to elect members of the European Parliament. There is an 'open' version of this system, but this is not used in the UK

Details of other systems

The supplementary vote

The SV system is used for electing the London mayor and other mayors.

Operation

Voters are given two choices, first and second.

If a candidate wins more than 50% of first-choice votes, he or she is elected. If not, all candidates drop out except the top two in the voting. Second preferences are added to first preferences and the winner now achieves a majority.

Impacts

The system ensures that the winner has an overall majority. It ensures fairness because all voters have two choices and so can potentially affect the outcome.

Table 20 Election for London mayor, 2008 (by supplementary vote)

Candidate	First-preference votes	Total first and second preferences
Boris Johnson (Con)	1.044 million	1.169 million (elected)
Ken Livingstone (Lab)	0.894 million	1.029 million
Brian Paddick (Lib Dem)	0.237 million (eliminated)	

The alternative vote

The AV system is not used, except for some by-elections in Scotland and Northern Ireland. It was rejected in the 2011 referendum on electoral reform.

Operation

The country is divided into constituencies, as under first-past-the-post. Each constituency returns one winner as MP.

Voters place all candidates in order of preference. (Voters do not have to vote for all candidates, but only as many as they wish.)

If one candidate wins more than 50% of first-preference votes, he or she is elected.

If no candidate achieves an overall majority of first choices, the lowest placed candidate is eliminated. His or her second-choice votes are distributed to the other candidates.

This process continues until one candidate has an overall majority.

Impacts

As the AV system has not been used in the UK, the potential impacts are uncertain. It is generally believed that there would be relatively little change from first-past-the-post. However, it is assumed that the Liberal Democrats would gain some seats at the expense of both main parties. Small parties would gain little if anything. Voters would have a greater choice and not need to vote tactically.

Additional member system

The additional member system (AMS) is used for electing the Scottish Parliament, Welsh Assembly and Greater London Assembly.

Operation

Most (about two-thirds) of the seats are elected by first-past-the-post. The rest of the seats are awarded by the regional list system.

Voters have two votes, one for first-past-the-post and the other on the regional list system.

The list system operates where each party offers a list of candidates for that region. Voters chose a party rather than an individual. Seats are awarded in proportion to the votes cast for each party in each region.

Examiner tip

Beware! The term 'proportional representation' is *not* an electoral system. It describes the characteristics of a number of systems which tend to produce proportional results. If you are asked what proportional representation is, you should explain it and use one or two systems only as examples.

Examiner tip

If you are asked to discuss and evaluate different electoral systems, consider two general aspects. First, how fair are they to voters and therefore how democratic are they? Second, what is the likely outcome in terms of the party system and government formation and its subsequent strength or weakness? Are such outcomes desirable or not?

The seats awarded on the list system are not in proportion to votes cast, but are distorted in favour of those parties that have been most disadvantaged in the constituency, first-past-the-post system. This is called the differential top-up system.

Impacts

There are two types of representative — those elected in constituencies and those elected by the list system.

The system increases voter choice, as voters have two votes.

It enables smaller parties, such as the Greens, to win some seats.

The overall outcome tends to be approximately proportional to support for all parties.

Before 2011, the system produced either minority or coalition governments because no party won an overall majority. However, in 2011 the Scottish National Party did win an overall majority in the Scottish Parliament, and Labour won exactly half the seats in Wales. We can now say that its impact on the main parties is unpredictable.

Table 21 Election to the Scottish Parliament, 2011 (additional member system)

Party	Votes (regional lists) (%)	Constituency seats	Regional list seats	Total seats	Seats (%)
Scottish National Party	44.0	53	16	69	53.5
Labour	26.3	15	22	37	28.7
Conservative	12.4	3	12	15	11.6
Lib Dem	5.2	2	3	5	3.9
Green	4.4	0	3	3	2.3
Total	92.3	73	56	129	100

Single transferable vote

The STV system is used for electing the Northern Ireland assembly and for local government in both Northern Ireland and Scotland.

Operation

Under this system there are multi-member constituencies. As it operates in the UK, each constituency returns six members.

Voters place candidates in order of preference and may vote for as many or few candidates as they wish.

Each party produces a list of its candidates in each constituency. This may be up to six, though in practice they rarely nominate more than three.

An electoral quota is calculated. This is the number of votes cast, divided by the number of seats plus one, and then one is added. Thus, if there are 50,000 votes and six seats, the quota is 50,000 divided by seven, plus one (= 7144).

The candidates who achieve the quota on first preferences are automatically elected.

Thereafter the surplus votes (above the quota) of wining candidates are taken and the second preferences added to other candidates until another candidate achieves the quota. The process is continued until six candidates achieve the quota.

Impacts

STV gives voters a large choice and allows them to show a preference between candidates of the same party.

Voters have a choice of six representatives when deciding whom they wish to pursue their grievances.

It helps small parties win seats.

The overall outcome is a multi-party system. In Northern Ireland, five different parties win a significant number of seats.

It favours a 'power-sharing system' where all parties have a place in the Assembly and in government. This is essential in a deeply divided society such as Northern Ireland.

Table 22 Election to the Northern Ireland Assembly, 2011 (STV)

Party	Votes won (first preference) (%)	Seats won	Seats won (%)
Democratic Unionist Party	29.3	38	35.2
Sinn Fein	26.3	29	26.9
Ulster Unionist Party	12.9	16	14.8
Social Democratic Labour Party	13.9	14	13.0
Alliance	7.5	8	7.4
Green	0.9	1	0.9
Others	9.2	2	1.9
Total	100	108	100

Regional list system (closed)

The closed regional list system is used for electing members of the European Parliament.

Operation

The country is divided into regions.

In each region parties create a list of candidates in their order of preference (this is the 'closed' variation — in the 'open' list system, the voters place candidates in their own order of preference).

Voters choose one of the party lists. In other words, they vote for a party rather than an individual candidate.

Seats are awarded in direct proportion to the number of votes cast. For example, if a party wins 30% of the votes in a region, it is awarded the top 30% of candidates on its list for that region.

The winning candidates represent a region rather than a constituency.

Impacts

There is a close correlation between the proportion of votes cast and seats awarded.

Every vote is of exactly equal value.

The system helps smaller parties such as the Green Party, the BNP and UKIP.

As it is not used in the UK to elect a government of any kind, the fact that a large number of parties wins seats is of relatively little significance. (In countries where this system is used to elect the main parliament and government, its impact is more significant and tends to produce multi-party systems and therefore coalitions.)

Table 23 Elections to the European Parliament, 2009 (regional list)

Party	Votes (%)	Seats won	Seats won (%)
Conservative	27.7	25	36.2
UKIP	16.5	13	18.9
Labour	15.7	13	18.9
Lib Dem	13.7	11	15.9
Green	8.1	2	2.9
BNP	6.2	2	2.9
Others	12.1	3	4.3
Total	100	69	100

Examiner tip

When describing and explaining different electoral systems, always give examples of their results and impact. You should use examples from the UK, including Scotland, Wales and Northern Ireland.

Party system

A description of a political system indicating approximately how many political parties gain significant representation and influence. The nature of party systems varies from single-dominant-party systems, two-party systems, through two-and-a-half-party systems to multi-party systems.

Electoral systems and party systems

The electoral systems described above give rise to different party systems. That is, they tend to result in a political system which is characterised by a particular number of parties. Party systems are described in Table 24. The types of electoral systems most likely to produce the various party systems are identified, together with some examples.

Table 24 Party systems and electoral systems

Party system	Associated electoral system(s)	Examples
One-dominant-party system One party is almost always in power, often in coalition with others. It occurs when there is a high level of consensus in a society and the party represents that consensus	This can occur with any electoral system	Japan (Liberal Democrats) Sweden (Social Democrats)
Two-party system Where only two parties have a realistic chance of gaining power	First-past-the-post. This is because this electoral system discriminates against smaller parties and presents most voters with a choice between two potential winners	The USA The UK

Party system	Associated electoral system(s)	Examples
Two-and-a half-party system A description often used of the UK, especially after 2010. It suggests that, while two parties dominate the system, there is a third party that has influence and may, as in 2010, actually hold the balance of power	First-past-the-post Additional member system (potentially) French second ballot system (not used in the UK and therefore not described here)	The UK France
Multi-party system Where more than two parties realistically compete for power	Additional member system STV Regional list	Scotland Wales Northern Ireland Italy The Netherlands

An evaluation of electoral reform

As part of the coalition agreement it was decided that a referendum would be held on changing the voting system for elections to the Westminster Parliament to the alternative vote (AV). On Thursday 5 May 2011 the referendum produced a clear result against this change: 67.9% (13 million) were against change, 32.1% (6 million) were in favour. This now in effect halts any possible electoral reform for a considerable period. However, we can still ascertain competing views about the suitability of first-past-the-post (FPTP) as used in the Westminster elections (see Tables 25 and 26).

Table 25 Should we continue with the first-past-the-post electoral voting system for Westminster elections? Reasons for saying YES

Simple to use	All that is required is one simple 'X' (cross) in a box. Few ballot papers are spoilt
Quick	Election results are obtained after just a few hours and new governments within 24 hours
Keeps out extremist parties	It prevents extremist parties gaining support and credibility which may undermine democratic values
Keeps a constituency link	Citizens can identify their representative and deal with issues directly with that person
Produces strong government	Governments with clear working majorities can achieve set goals and fulfil their manifesto pledges
Produces stable government	Governments are not undermined by coalition deals which can create insecurity and they can serve a full term in office
Clear accountability	There are clear lines of responsibility for the government. It can take the praise if its actions are successful and the blame if things go wrong. If it is the latter, the FPTP system has a sense of punishing a government that lets the public down

Electoral reform
A belief that, or set of proposals as to how, the system of elections should be changed. This may be limited to changes in details such as who is entitled to vote, how votes should be cast (for example, internet voting etc.). It more usually means proposals to change the overall system of converting votes into seats, for example from first-past-the-post to AV or to proportional representation.

Strong government
A term implying that a government is able to act decisively; is unlikely to encounter excessive opposition which will hamper its progress; and is usually able to drive its measures though Parliament without undue delay or obstruction.

Stable government
The term used to describe a circumstance where the government of the day is unlikely to become disunited or even to fall from power imminently. This implies that, once elected, a government will serve its full term of office of 5 years (Westminster Parliament).

Reflects broad popular movements	The general elections of 1979 and 1997 were seen as representing a 'sea change' or major shift in public opinion; the FPTP system can reflect this prevailing mood
Poor alternatives on offer	No system which has gained widespread support and can deliver the benefits of FPTP has yet been presented to the public
No demand for change	The outcome of the referendum on 5 May ended any question that the current system was unpopular and that change was desired

Table 26 Should we continue with the first-past-the-post electoral voting system for Westminster elections? Reasons for saying NO

Lack of legitimacy of MPs	Less than one-third of MPs get 50% of the vote in their constituency
Lack of legitimacy of government	No single-party government in the UK since 1931 has won over 50% of the vote. Governments are formed with a minority of the votes cast. This fell as low as 35% for Labour in 2005
Unfair to small parties	Small parties are unfairly punished by the FPTP system and get nowhere near their share of the seats. The Liberal Democrats got 8.7% of the seats for 23% of the vote in 2010
Bias to large parties	As small parties suffer, so the bigger parties dominate, which means that FPTP ensures it is a two-party race for government
Bias to Labour	Labour enjoys an unfair bias as it has the lowest vote-to-seat ratio — it takes fewer votes to elect a Labour MP than any other MP
May 2010	May 2010 shows how the FPTP system cannot cope if there are more than two contenders. The system could not accommodate the complexities of a multi-party system and deliver a fair outcome
Wasted votes	Millions of votes go to elect nobody. These are votes for candidates who have no chance of winning, or votes in safe seats where the result is never in doubt
Safe seats — electoral deserts	Few seats change hands in elections. General elections are decided in the marginal seats. This means not all votes are of equal value In areas where the outcome is so predictable as to be a foregone conclusion, to vote for any alternative may be seen as pointless — thus apathy wins, as people see their vote as counting for nothing
Poor social representation	The current FPTP system produces a narrow range of politicians with little social reflection. When alternative electoral systems (especially proportional representation systems) are introduced, this dramatically improves

The general election of May 2010

Table 27 shows the results of the election of May 2010. Below the table are some key facts which may be used to illustrate answers to questions concerning the first-past-the-post electoral system and electoral reform.

Table 27 Results of the May 2010 general election

Party	Seats won	Total votes won	Percentage of votes won	Percentage of seats won
Conservative	307	10,726,614	36.1	47.2
Labour	258	8,609,527	29.0	39.6
Liberal Democrat	57	6,836,824	23.0	8.7
Democratic Unionist Party	8	168,216	0.6	1.2
Scottish National Party	6	491,386	1.7	0.9
Sinn Fein	5	171,942	0.6	0.8
Plaid Cymru	3	165,394	0.6	0.5
Social Democratic & Labour Party	3	110,970	0.4	0.5
Green Party	1	285,616	1.0	0.2
Alliance Party	1	42,762	0.1	0.2
UK Independence Party (UKIP)	0	919,546	3.1	0
British National Party (BNP)	0	564,331	1.9	0
Others	1	598,252	1.9	0.2
Total	650	29,691,380	Turnout: 65.2%	

Key facts concerning the results of the 2010 general election

- No party managed to win 326 seats, which would have delivered a single party majority. The result was a hung parliament.
- The two main parties (Labour and the Conservatives) collectively polled their lowest share of the vote since the Second World War.
- The Conservative Party and the Liberal Democrats formed a coalition — the first since the Second World War.
- The pre-election campaign included the first ever televised debates between the party leaders.
- One condition of the coalition agreement was a national referendum on changing the first-past-the-post voting system to the alternative vote. The proposal to change the system was rejected in the 2011 referendum.
- Only one-third of MPs secured 50% of the vote in their constituencies.
- The Green Party saw the election of their first ever MP.
- The results continue to discriminate against the Liberal Democrats, who gained only 8.7% of the seats for 23% of the vote.

Knowledge check 15

What do the results of the 2010 general election tell us about the first-past-the-post electoral system?

- Knowledge and understanding of where and when elections take place in the UK
- Knowledge and understanding of the functions of elections
- Knowledge and understanding of the key terms associated with electoral systems
- Knowledge and explanation of how elections are connected to the concept of democracy
- Knowledge and understanding of the concepts of simple plurality, majoritarian and proportional electoral systems
- Understanding of how all the various electoral systems used in the UK operate
- Explanation of why new electoral systems were introduced in the UK since 1997
- Distinction between majoritarian and proportional representation
- Comparison and evaluation of how different electoral systems can and do produce different outcomes

- Critical evaluatation of the advantages and disadvantages of the electoral system used to elect MPs to Westminster
- Knowledge and analysis of the case for electoral reform for Westminster elections
- Definitions of and distinction between a party manifesto and a mandate
- Understanding and evaluation of the significance and implications of the most recent election results in the UK and the most recent general election results
- Knowledge and understanding of the various categories of party system
- Analysis and evaluation of which party system is most appropriate for the UK
- Analysis and evaluation of the importance of and impact of the referendum on changing the voting system held in May 2011

Pressure groups

What is a pressure group?

Examiner tip

When answering a question about pressure groups, ensure that you use real-world examples to illustrate your answer.

A pressure group is an organised group of people, united by a common cause or topic, who wish to influence and change the policies and views of government. They also seek to influence and change the opinions and views of the general public. Pressure groups have become a central feature of representative democracies; their presence in other counties is seen as a sign of an open and progressive democracy, while restrictions placed on pressure groups by other regimes are seen as repressive and undemocratic.

Classification of pressure groups

The specification stresses two ways of classifying pressure groups. The first divides them into sectional or promotional groups. The second differentiates between insiders and outsiders. The meaning of these classifications is set out below.

Sectional/promotional groups

Sectional groups

Sectional groups are sometimes described as 'interest groups' or 'protective groups'. Such a group is defined by a common uniting feature of the group members. Often the uniting feature will be economic interests, but sectional groups can also represent social groups or those who have some other common interest, such as sufferers from a particular disease. Here are some useful examples of sectional groups:

- **Unite** — Britain's biggest trade union, representing general workers
- **FBU** — the Fire Brigades' Union
- **NFU** — the National Farmers' Union, representing farming interests
- **Taxpayers' Alliance** — looking after the interests of all who pay taxes
- **AA** — Automobile Association, representing the interests of motorists
- **Age UK** — concerned with the interests of the elderly
- **the Multiple Sclerosis Society** — representing sufferers, carers and researchers
- **CBI** — the Confederation of British Industry, representing many British businesses
- **Forest** — defends the rights and interests of tobacco smokers

Sectional groups like those shown above tend to be self-interested in that they are mainly concerned with their own interest. However, sometimes, as with teachers' unions, they believe that the interests of their members and those of society as a whole are the same.

Promotional groups

Promotional groups are sometimes known as 'issue groups' or 'cause groups'. Such groups are defined by commonly-held beliefs or causes. The uniting feature may take many forms; it could be the cause of wildlife, the environment or child welfare. Promotional groups tend to be interested in the interests of the whole community, not merely a section of the community, as is the case with sectional groups. Some prominent examples of promotional groups are:

- **Friends of the Earth** — campaigning on a range of issues concerning environmental protection
- **Greenpeace** — similar to Friends of the Earth, but tending to be more militant
- **ASH** — Action on Smoking and Health, dedicated to reducing the use of tobacco in society
- **Liberty** — a campaign group interested in strengthening individual rights and liberties
- **UK Uncut** — a loose campaign group drawing attention to individuals and businesses who avoid paying UK taxes
- **the RSPCA** — concerned with animal welfare issues

It should be noted that some pressure groups do not fit exactly into either the sectional or promotional category. These are groups that represent both a section of society and an issue. For example, the **NSPCC** campaigns against child cruelty generally and represents the interests of children in danger. Similarly, **Plane Stupid** is a federation of protest groups that seek to stop airport expansions. They do this both as an environmental issue and to defend the interests of those who would be adversely affected by such expansions.

Insider/outsider groups

This definition or distinction was created by Wyn Grant and considers pressure groups from the perspective of their relationship with the political establishment, the government and civil service. To some extent, it explains how pressure groups behave, and also whether they are successful or otherwise.

Insider pressure groups

An insider group is defined as having a close and established working relationship with government. This in a sense confers a type of legitimacy or acceptance on the group and it is seen to be an advantage. There are various ways in which groups may gain insider status. These include the following:

- They may have a close relationship with a government department and/or ministers and so be consulted regularly. This is particularly important if they are involved in the early development and drafting of legislation. Such groups are called 'core insiders' because of their special status.
- They may have representatives on permanent policy-advising committees.
- They may be regularly consulted by parliamentary select committees of MPs.
- They may have institutional links with a political party, as unions have with the Labour Party.
- The EU keeps a register of pressure groups which have special access to the policy-making European Commission and the European Parliament.

Examples of insider pressure groups in 2011 are:

- **BMA** — the British Medical Association, advised the coalition government on NHS reform issues
- **NFU** — consulted by both the British government and the EU on issues such as farm subsidies and agricultural policy
- **CBI** — reports regularly to government on the state of British business
- **the RSPCA** — consults with ministers and Parliament on animal welfare
- **ASH** — involved in the drafting of anti-smoking legislation

Outsider pressure groups

Outsider groups by contrast have no established working patterns or productive links with government. They are seen as outside the decision-making framework of governments and are not consulted. They are less likely to have their views taken into account. This may make it more difficult for outsiders to achieve success.

Outsiders may have that status for a number of reasons. It may be that they are not established enough, they may not wish to be insiders because that would limit their independence or they may not wish to be accountable for their actions. Outsiders have greater freedom to act as they wish, including acts of civil disobedience.

Examples of classic outsider groups are the following:

- **Greenpeace** — specialises in acts of disobedience such as destroying genetically modified (GM) crops and obstructing whaling ships
- **Plane Stupid** — also uses civil disobedience to obstruct plans to expand airports

Examiner tip
If you are asked to describe different types or classifications of pressure groups, you can use either sectional/promotional or insiders/outsiders or both.

- **Unlock Democracy** — campaigns for constitutional reform; not accepted by government as a legitimately representative organisation
- **Taxpayers' Alliance** — a relatively new group, which tends to be hostile to government, so is not granted insider status

The functions of pressure groups

Pressure groups have various functions.

- Sectional groups act to protect and safeguard the interests of their members; this is most clear with professional groups and trade unions. They can provide a range of services. A trade union will protect the worker in the workplace from employer harassment; the British Medical Association acts to offer the latest advice to GPs in running their practices.
- Pressure groups offer a means of representation which supplements the electoral system. Thus pressure groups can speak up for minorities such as AIDS victims or, as in the case of Age UK, victims of problems with pensions.
- Pressure groups inform and educate. They aim to keep the general public up to date with key issues by explaining events and offering warnings. For example, Greenpeace constantly measures levels of radioactive pollution around UK nuclear power plants; the environmental organisation WWF regularly publishes articles such as its 'Living Planet Report' on the state of biodiversity in the world.
- Pressure groups help governments make decisions. On specialist areas a government will consult particular pressure groups for their expertise. If a major initiative takes place in agriculture, for example, the UK government will consult the NFU. Similarly, the NFU worked with the government when the foot and mouth disease crisis engulfed the UK. If child welfare law is reformed, the government will work with the NSPCC.
- Pressure groups are a mechanism for political expression and participation between elections. For example, the marches in London in March 2011 by trade union groups were expressions of dissatisfaction with the coalition government's programme of public spending cutbacks

Distinctions between pressure groups and political parties

An understanding of the functions of pressure groups can be improved by considering how they differ from political parties. The key differences are as follows:

- The main distinction is that parties seek to gain power; they are hoping to become the government or achieve a share in government. Pressure groups do not have that aspiration. They seek to influence but not to govern.
- Closely related to that difference is the fact that pressure groups are concerned with a relatively narrow range of issues, sometimes only one issue. Because they seek governmental power, however, parties must develop policies across the whole range of government business. For example, the Green Party in Britain began life as an environmental pressure group with only environmental issues on its agenda.

Knowledge check 16

Briefly explain any three distinctions between insider and outsider pressure groups.

Examiner tip

If you are asked to describe the main functions of pressure groups, try to put the functions in some sort of order of importance. The order shown here is a good guide to this.

When it became a party and sought to gain election for its representatives, it had to develop policies on the economy, foreign affairs, welfare, law and order etc.

- A third important factor flows from the above two. Since parties are seeking governmental power, they must accept the need to be accountable for their policies. They cannot consider a few issues in isolation; they must judge how all their policies might affect the government of the country or locality. Pressure groups, on the other hand, do not have to be accountable and so can campaign on their issues, or for their section of society, without concerning themselves with their impact on the rest of government policy.
- It is normal for parties to have a formal organisation. They need to develop political programmes, organise campaigning and select candidates for office. Pressure groups may have a formal organisation, but many do not and none has to be as organised as a political party.

It is important to understand that there are some ways in which the distinctions are blurred. There may be overlaps between the functions of pressure groups and those of political parties. Examples of this blurring are as follows:

- Some pressure groups offer candidates for election at local and national level as a way of publicising an issue. The anti-abortion 'Right to Life' campaign, for example, has sought election for a few candidates. However, this does not mean that the group is seeking power.
- Some parties are so narrow in their aims that they look more like pressure groups. It could be argued that the UK Independence Party (UKIP) does not seek power, but tries to put pressure on other parties, especially the Conservatives, from whom they may attract votes on issues such as opposition to the EU, mass immigration and devolution. Similarly, the BNP has no prospect of power, but campaigns on issues such as immigration and anti-multiculturalism.
- Pressure groups often transform themselves into parties. This is how the Green Party came about, while UKIP began life as a single-issue anti-EU movement.

Knowledge check 17

Explain why the distinction between pressure groups and parties may be unclear.

Pressure group methods and objectives

Whatever the methods they employ, pressure groups are seeking to achieve a number of objectives:

- to influence policy and decision makers at all appropriate levels of government, from local level to regional, national and European levels
- as part of the above, to sponsor new policies and legislation, to prevent unfriendly legislation from being implemented or to amend proposed legislation to make it more friendly to the group's cause or the section of society it represents
- to bring issues to the public attention, to force these issues onto the 'political agenda'
- to mobilise public support for their issues or causes, and thus put pressure on decision makers
- to defend the legal rights of their members

In order to achieve these objectives, pressure groups use a variety of methods. These vary according to the objective they are pursuing. Table 28 matches typical pressure group methods with objectives and identifies some important examples.

Table 28 Pressure group methods

Objective	Typical method(s)	Examples
To influence policy and decision makers	Seek insider status As insiders, lobby ministers, MPs and peers Seek to be involved in the development of policy and legislation Seek to influence party policy makers	National Farmers' Union Confederation of British Industry Royal College of Nursing Mencap Adam Smith Institute (pro free markets)
To achieve friendly legislation, prevent unfriendly legislation, promote amendments to legislation	Give evidence to parliamentary select and legislative committees Seek places on policy-making and legislation-drafting committees	Action on Smoking and Health (ASH) British Bankers' Association. (BBA) British Beer and Pub Association
To raise public awareness and place issues on the public agenda	Organise publicity campaigns in the media Organise large demonstrations Internet campaigns and e-petitions Publicity stunts	Greenpeace Taxpayers' Alliance RSPCA Liberty UK Uncut
To mobilise public opinion to pressurise government	Organise public demonstrations Engage in mass civil disobedience Involve celebrities and 'big names'	National Union of Students (tuition fees) Trade unions (public sector expenditure cuts) Anti-Tesco expansion groups Plane Stupid
To pursue the legal rights of members	Appeals and judicial reviews in the courts to establish rights which are threatened	Trade unions Stonewall (gay rights) Age UK

The power and influence of pressure groups

Pressure group power, as well as pressure group success and failure, are crucial areas to cover. It is vital that you are familiar with the key concepts of pluralism and elitism. Table 29 considers pressure groups in relation to each of these concepts.

Knowledge check 18

Explain briefly three ways in which the methods of insider and outsider pressure groups differ.

Pluralism The belief that power is evenly and widely spread in society. Many pressure groups can and do contribute to the political process and this is a positive thing. There is open access to information and dialogue and discourse flourishes.

Elitism The belief that power is restricted and narrowly dispersed. Few pressure groups contribute to the political process and this is a negative characteristic. Access to information and the decision-making process is withheld from many.

Table 29 Do pressure groups demonstrate pluralism or elitism?

Evidence for pluralism	Evidence for elitism
There are numerous pressure groups and no restrictions on formation	There may be numerous pressure groups but only a few really matter
It is increasingly easy to express pressure group views	Information is still restricted and some groups have access to more information than others; information is power
Governments listen to pressure groups and act on their concerns	Governments have agendas of their own. They can and do choose to ignore many pressure groups. The notion of a neutral pressure group is false
No pressure group is so powerful that it dominates all others; there is a lot of parity between the groups	Some pressure groups are so strong they dominate the political environment
It is possible that some pressure groups will succeed as others fail, for they advance their argument in a competitive environment	Only a small elite number of pressure groups will succeed
Taken together, the above means that power is dispersed and shared out in society; participation is increased	Taken together, the above means that power is restricted and held by the few; participation is limited

Examiner tip

When discussing pressure group success, it is good practice to explain first what 'success' may mean.

What factors determine pressure group success?

The key factors that determine pressure group success are outlined in Table 30. In each case, examples are given to illustrate the feature.

Table 30 Pressure group success

Factor	Pressure group	Evidence of success
Resources — financial and organisational, giving a group the ability and personnel to mount a major campaign	Countryside Alliance — organised mass demonstrations in London	The 'watering down' of anti-foxhunting legislation in 2004
Insider status — being established in government circles and well trusted	Action on Smoking and Health	A series of pieces of legislation to deter and reduce smoking
Tactics — groups may find a good formula for influencing government and/or mobilising public support	The Save England's Forests Campaign used a variety of tactics, including a huge e-petition, celebrity campaigners, demonstrations and MP involvement	The cancellation of government plans to sell off large quantities of publicly owned forest in 2010
Sharing the same agenda as the government — this is a significant help when campaigning for change	Confederation of British Industry — welcomed a new business-friendly government in 2010	A commitment by government to reduce corporation tax on company profits by 14% over 4 years
Lack of opposition	Make Poverty History, a campaign group of the 1990s and the first decade of the twenty-first century, experienced little opposition to its championing of developing countries	Government commitments to raise foreign debt relief and increase overseas aid
Favourable circumstances	Action on Smoking and Health was helped by reductions in cases of lung cancer following anti-smoking legislation	A ban on smoking in public places in England and Wales secured by ASH in 2006

Factor	Pressure group	Evidence of success
Celebrity involvement	The Gurkha Justice Campaign led by actress Joanna Lumley demanded that retired Gurkhas (Nepalese troops serving in the British army) should have the right to settle in Britain	The campaign was a huge success and the government was forced, in 2009, to reverse its policies denying Gurkhas the right to stay in Britain
Strategic position	The British Bankers' Association (BBA) used its representation of powerful banks to campaign against banking reform. The government feared that large banks might move away from Britain if their operations were curbed	A dilution of plans to limit banks' awards of excessive bonuses and high salaries in 2011

The importance of pressure groups

Table 31 evaluates the extent to which pressure groups have grown in importance.

Table 31 Have pressure groups become more important in recent years?

Yes	No
They have increased in number and range	An increase in numbers may be as a result of splitting an issue, with a separate pressure group for each stance, e.g., pro- and anti-abortion groups Too many groups may dilute the messages people can become involved with and overwhelm the political stage
Their membership has increased far above that of political parties. Party membership has declined dramatically since the 1980s, while membership of pressure groups is growing	Size and membership may be important but whereas political parties hold real power, pressure groups can only influence the political process
Their profile is now constantly in the media and more people are aware of them	Greater media profile and increased public awareness could lead to information overload, and may produce passive involvement as people feel that they take part just by viewing media information
The public seek political change and redress through pressure groups before any other avenue	The public may seek change and redress through pressure groups, but it is government who has the final say and it will put its self-interest first
They have achieved notable successes	Far more pressure groups have failed than have been successful
There is an increasing number of access points to connect with a pressure group	The increase in access points is not necessarily a sign of success

Knowledge check 19

Choose three important pressure groups and explain briefly how and why they have been successful.

Pressure groups and democracy

Pressure groups are seen as a major contributor to how democracy functions in the UK. Opinions are divided as to whether they support or damage democracy.

Examiner tip

Probably the most important aspect of the relationship between pressure groups and democracy is the degree to which pressure groups disperse or concentrate power. Remember to express this idea when evaluating pressure groups.

Ways in which pressure groups enhance democracy

- Pressure groups often represent groups and causes that have been ignored by political parties.
- They help to disperse power more widely, preventing dangerous concentrations of power.
- They help to educate and inform the public about important issues.
- They may help the governing process by providing informed advice.
- They can act as a control mechanism against overmighty government.
- They provide ways in which people can participate in politics, especially at a time when traditional forms of participation are declining.
- They provide an outlet for public grievances, a process known as 'tension release'.

Ways in which pressure groups do *not* support democracy

- Pressure groups may undermine the authority of elected officials and Parliament.
- They can be seen as the 'politics of self-interest' and may present the public with overbiased or even false information.
- If they are too powerful they may create so-called 'hyperpluralism', which can hold up the process of government by being too obstructive.
- Pressure groups lack elective legitimacy and are not democratically accountable.
- Those that engage in civil disobedience threaten order in society and subvert democracy.
- Some wealthy or influential pressure groups may have more influence than can be justified.
- The leadership of some elitist groups may not reflect accurately the views of their memberships.

Knowledge check 20

Explain three ways in which pressure groups are 'good for democracy'.

Knowledge summary

- Knowledge and understanding of how pressure groups are classified
- Knowledge and understanding of the features and characteristics of pressure groups
- Knowledge and explanation of the functions of pressure groups in a representative democracy
- Knowledge and understanding of several pressure groups, with a brief profile of their structure, member profile, aims and political outcomes
- Comparison of pressure groups with political parties, how and why they are alike and how and why they differ
- Understanding of how pressure groups work with political parties, both in and out of government
- Knowledge and analysis of the methods and tactics used by groups and the impact that this has in terms of outcomes

- Analysis and appreciation as to whether pressure groups are becoming more or less important in the UK
- Understanding and evaluation of how the fortunes of pressure groups may change over time
- Knowledge and understanding of the key terms pluralism and elitism and how they relate to pressure group power
- Analysis and evaluation of why some pressure groups are more successful than others
- Analysis and evaluation of the relationship of pressure groups to representative democracy and consideration of the positive and negative implications
- Analysis and evaluation of the concept of pluralist democracy and how this applies to pressure-group activity

Questions & Answers

How to use this section

At the beginning of this section there is a guide to the structure of the examination for Unit 1, followed by an explanation of the assessment objectives and a guide as to how the marks for each assessment objective are distributed among the different questions on the paper. It is important that you familiarise yourself with all three of these features — the exam structure, the nature of assessment objectives and how you can score marks for each of those assessment objectives.

There follow some specimen examination questions. These are neither past examination questions, nor future examination questions, but they are very similar to the kind of questions you will face.

The best way to use this section of the guide is to look at each question and make notes on how you would go about answering it, including the key facts and knowledge you would use, relevant examples, the analysis, arguments and evaluations you would deploy and the conclusions you would reach. You should also make a plan of how you would answer the whole question, taking into account the examiner tip (indicated by the icon ⊜) immediately below the question.

After each specimen question there are two exemplar answers. One will be a strong answer and the other will be either weak or of medium quality. The strength of each specimen answer is indicated in the examiner commentary (again indicated by the icon ⊜) that follows it. In the commentary there are also notes on the answer's strengths and weaknesses and an indication as to how marks would be awarded for each assessment objective. Now compare these specimen answers with your own notes. Amend your notes to bring them to the standard of the stronger specimen. Having done all this, you can now attempt a full answer to the question, aiming to avoid the weaknesses and include the strengths that have been indicated in the specimen answers and explanations of the marks.

Of course you may use the information in your own way. The above guidance is merely a recommendation. Remember, however, that simply 'learning' the strong specimen answers will not help — these are answers to specimen questions, not to the questions you will actually face. It is preferable to learn how to answer questions 'actively', that is by writing your own answers, using the questions and answers as a guide. In this way you will be able to tackle effectively any questions that may come your way in the examination.

The structure of the examination

The examination is made up of four questions, each of which has the same structure. You are required to answer just *two* of these questions. There is no restriction on which two you choose. There will be one question on each of the four sections of the specification. In other words, all four specification sections will appear on the paper.

Individual questions will not, however, require specific knowledge from more than one specification section (though candidates may bring in relevant knowledge to their answers from any part of the specification). The time allowed is 40 minutes for each question: 1 hour and 20 minutes for the whole examination. Students are advised to divide their time equally between the two questions selected. *It is a general principle that students are expected to spend about 1 minute of their time for each mark available.* So, for a 5-mark question, use 5 minutes, for a 10-mark question, use 10 minutes, and for a 25-mark question, use 25 minutes.

The questions are all divided into three parts — (a), (b) and (c).

Part (a) may be asking for a definition of a concept or a key term, often requiring an example in back-up. Part (a) carries 5 marks.

Part (b) is again asking for your understanding and knowledge of a particular area. It may ask for three distinct points. Once again, the use of examples will be beneficial in detailing that exposure. Part (b) carries 10 marks.

Part (c) carries the most marks. This is the most difficult section of the question. It has a base of knowledge but then calls for deeper academic skills, such as the ability to offer criticism and evaluation. In simple terms, you are asked to validate or reject arguments which have more than one viewpoint: in essence this is the nature of politics — the controversy and debate which surrounds controversial issues and themes. Part (c) carries 25 marks.

The nature of assessment objectives

There are three assessment objectives, described in the table below. Assessment objectives have two purposes. First, they are a guide for students, demonstrating the kind of knowledge, understanding and skills they need to do well in the examination. Second, they are a guide to those who will mark the examination. Markers do not merely give marks for their overall impression of an answer. Instead they mark 'by assessment objective'. This means that they may award marks for up to three separate assessment objectives. Thus a candidate may do well on assessment objectives 1 and 2 but poorly on 3, or well on all three, or poorly on them all. Markers must 'dissect' an answer to decide how well a candidate has been able to meet each of the assessment objectives.

These are the descriptions of the three assessment objectives published by Edexcel, which sets and organises the marking of this Unit:

Assessment objective	Skills required
AO1	Demonstrate knowledge and understanding of relevant institutions, processes, political concepts, theories and debates
AO2	Analyse and evaluate political information, arguments and explanations, and identify parallels, connections, similarities and differences between the aspects of the political systems studied
AO3	Construct and communicate coherent arguments making use of a range of appropriate political vocabulary

To give an idea of what these mean in practice, we may consider a topic and look at typical knowledge and skills required:

Democracy

AO1

- How is democracy defined?
- What categories of democracy apply in the UK?
- What is the difference between direct and representative democracy?
- What features of the UK's democratic system can you identify?
- What strengths can you identify in the UK's democratic system?
- What weaknesses can you identify in the UK's democratic system?
- How and where have referendums been used in the UK?
- What improvements have been suggested to develop democracy in the UK?

AO2

- Why have problems emerged in democracy in the UK?
- Are these problems solvable?
- What issues arise with the suggested solutions to democracy in the UK?
- Why have they been supported or opposed?
- What impact have changes recently introduced made to democracy in the UK?
- What are the prospects for further reform?

AO3

- Use of appropriate political vocabulary such as legitimacy, democratic deficit, initiatives, modernisation, apathy, declining turnout
- Structure of the answer, including a logical introduction, clearly explained content and a reasoned conclusion, supported by evidence

We can further explain the use of assessment objectives by adding the following:

AO1 involves the knowledge of facts, key recent historical developments, how institutions work, how institutions are connected and interact, how institutions have changed and evolved, examples to illustrate theories, explanations of the main arguments for and against an issue.

AO2 involves explaining why certain developments have taken place, linkages between cause and effect, evaluations such as 'to what extent' or 'how much?', analysis of the relationships between political opinion and political changes, explanations and explorations of the relationships between institutions.

AO3 means clarity of meaning, use of vocabulary and structure of answer. Spelling and handwriting are of relatively minor importance as long as poor spelling or handwriting does not make meanings unclear.

The distribution of assessment objectives

Different questions and parts of questions carry a different distribution of assessment objective marks. It is important to be familiar with these as it should affect the way you answer a particular question. The distribution is as follows:

Part (a) 5-mark question: all 5 marks for AO1

Part (b) 10-mark question: 7 marks for AO1, 3 marks for AO2

Part (c) 25-mark question: 8 marks for AO1, 9 marks for AO2, 8 marks for AO3

Some features of this distribution should be emphasised:

Part (a) of each question carries marks *only* under AO1, for knowledge and understanding. Thus, you should stick to facts and knowledge and not attempt any analysis or evaluation. Though there are no marks under AO3 for communication, you should still write as clearly as possible.

Most of the marks for Part (b) questions are for AO1, but there are some AO2 marks. These are normally for making explanations, cause and effect and some analysis of processes and reasons for change.

Part (c) assessment objectives are evenly spread. Make sure you do undertake analysis and/or evaluation as this is nearly one-third of the marks. Also, take special care over the structure of your answer as well as your clarity and use of vocabulary.

Question 1 Democracy and political participation

(a) Using an example, define the term legitimacy. (5 marks)

ⓔ 'Legitimacy' is a key term on the specification and should be covered. Examples do not have to be exclusively provided from the UK. The example used should bring clarity to the concept.

Student A

Legitimacy is a term which is connected to rightfulness and correctness. **a** Legitimacy gives a political action justified authority; it presents the notion that the action is acceptable and permissible through agreed and acknowledged procedures. **b** By contrast, if a political action is deemed to be illegitimate, then this is seen as unfair and lacking in authority, and may be viewed as wrong. **c** Legitimacy can be exampled in a democratic system through elections. A government can claim that its actions are legitimate as the electorate has given it their support.

ⓔ **4/5 marks awarded.** This is a clear response. **a** First there is a precise definition, then the example is equally clearly set out. **b** Note how it is possible to define a term by reference to its opposite: here the contrast with illegitimacy is pertinent and useful. **c** The example of elections is one of many which could be called upon; sourcing from a codified (or uncodified) constitution would serve just as well. It is true that more could be developed but this is enough to reach high marks in the allocated time span. This answer achieves a grade A.

Student B

Legitimacy gives people a right to do something and they have to obey. **a** Often those in authority have legitimacy and can force people to do things they would not otherwise do. A good example of legitimacy is the police forcing an arrest on a burglar suspected of having carried out a crime. **b**

ⓔ **2/5 marks awarded.** This is quite a brief response and lacks precision and clarity. **a** There is confusion between the terms legitimacy and power. **b** Similarly, the example is not really 'political' in the sense we are looking for. The answer receives a grade C.

(b) Explain three characteristics which establish the UK's claim to democratic status. (10 marks)

ⓔ The term 'characteristics' has a similar meaning to 'features'. The question is searching for three things which the UK political system does which would be associated with democracy, and evidence that each of those things is in place. Try to ensure that the three things you choose are illustrated clearly with examples, as this question is asking you to do more than simply define a concept. The AO2 mark earned is determined by how clear your explanation is.

Student A

There is no doubt that the UK is entitled to claim democratic status and it can do this via several routes. Democracy has emerged slowly and steadily in the UK over the past 100 years. The most obvious claim to democratic status arises from the regular holding of elections to secure representatives and office holders. A general election for instance must take place at least every 5 years. Furthermore the general election (and all others) are subject to close scrutiny and official procedures and process, the casting of the vote must be in secret, the TV media has not to show any bias to a particular party and importantly the counting of the votes is done under close scrutiny. There are other significant processes which have to be followed to ensure that elections follow strict democratic procedures. **a** Secondly, in addition to elections there have been several referendums in the UK in recent years. There have been two national referendums: one over continued membership of the current EU and one to decide if we should change the way by which we elect Westminster MPs. Other referendums have taken place to decide if devolution of power was to take place in Scotland, Wales and Northern Ireland. Referendums are a link to the principle of direct democracy and can be said to motivate the public on crucial issues and stabilise the democratic process. In the UK they are now seen as essential if a government is to embark on major constitutional change. **b** Finally, the UK can claim democratic status as the country adheres to the principles associated with liberal democracy, which enshrines the principle and practice of civil liberties. Civil liberties are where the citizen is allowed particular rights or entitlements which the state cannot take away. There are several of these but one in particular which demonstrates clearly the UK's democratic status is freedom of association. This allows the citizen to form groups (political and otherwise) and take collective views and possibly actions. The ability to form pressure groups is a good example of this civil liberty, but perhaps even clearer for the UK's democratic status is the ability to form political parties and contest elections. Freedom of association allows new political parties to emerge and contest elections. The political party Respect formed in opposition to the Iraq war; while James Goldsmith was instrumental in the formation of the Referendum Party in the 1990s. **c**

e **10/10 marks awarded:** 7/7 for AO1, 3/3 for AO2. This response is really well focused and has the question clearly in target. There is a brief opening, which strictly speaking is not essential in a 10-mark question but it does set the scene. Three points are well developed. The use of examples in each not only enhances the knowledge and understanding (AO1), it also serves as a platform for AO2. **a** Elections are well explained and detailed. **b** Next the topic of referendums is well handled and finally **c** the introduction of civil liberties and the link with liberal democracy is excellent. In the time restrictions, little more could be expected and the answer earns full marks and hence an A grade.

Student B

Without doubt the UK is a democratic country and has been so for over hundreds of years. **a** The UK has numerous elections and these can be used to provide a choice of parties which if elected can put the views and opinions of the majority into operation. The elections are free and fair and anyone can stand for election. Anyone over 18 can vote in elections and these are held at regular intervals. Political parties explain prior to the election what they will propose to do and if a party is successful it claims a mandate to act on what it considers to be its victorious proposals. **b** As noted we have had these elections for centuries and these have established democracy in the UK. **c** Secondly, there is widespread participation and people can take part in politics however they choose. Millions of people have the opportunity to voice their feelings. They can join pressure groups and political parties and there are thousands who are members of pressure groups. The internet has allowed participation even more and made the UK even more democratic. **d** Finally, people are free and can say whatever they want without being arrested. These freedoms have been set out in laws which are available to protect us. This means that newspapers act as a democratic voice to uphold freedom and publicity. The UK has a wide range of newspapers, magazines and also the television, which can voice opposition and alternative views. **e**

ⓔ **5/10 marks awarded:** 4/7 for AO1 and 1/3 for AO2. This does raise at least three claims to democratic status for the UK. However, the response is at times ambiguous and not clear. It is prone to making generalisations, which are not supported. It is far better to provide one accurate and definite example than make generic points which have little empirical foundation. **a c** For instance the opening remark about centuries of democracy, repeated in the middle of the answer, is misleading. Democracy has evolved in the UK but it is a continual process. The democracy we enjoy now was not in place centuries ago — for instance women only got the vote on equal terms with men in 1928, less than 100 years ago. **b** Elections are the most obvious point to link the UK with democratic status, but the explanations and the development are not complete; despite this it is perhaps the best explained of all the three points developed. **d** The next topic, participation, is a good point to follow but it is again poorly developed. There is a note of pressure groups (which could be a point in itself) but the impact of this is lost. It requires definition, such as freedom of expression and freedom of association — both points which are hinted at but not fully defined. **e** The final category concerns civil liberties, a hallmark of liberal democracy, but it is not made explicit and clear. The response knows how to link the UK with democratic status but fails to capitalise on the knowledge. The AO2 is weak, the AO1 adequate. Overall the answers achieves no more than a grade C.

(c) How and why should democracy be enhanced in the UK?   (25 marks)

ⓔ 'How' and 'why' are crucial words here. The 'how' is the basis of the AO1 marks; you have to prove methods which can be introduced to make UK democracy better. The 'why' is the basis of the AO2 marks; here you need to justify why democracy is in need of renovation and upgrading.

Student A

There have been growing voices proclaiming that there is an urgent need to enhance and improve democracy in the UK. The UK is an indirect democracy and calls have been made to make this system operate in a fairer and more equitable fashion. This includes calls to change the operation of the representative model by changing the existing fabric. More radical alternatives by providing closer links with direct democracy have been called for. Both avenues of repair and renewal should be considered and evaluated as to their application. **a**

The current system of democracy suffers from defects in the electoral system which is used. This is most serious in how we elect MPs to Westminster using first-past-the-post. It is a non-proportional system and has a host of problems which include the dominance of safe seats, and the overimportance of marginal seats which are few in number but decide the outcome in a general election. This gives credence to the view that all votes are not of equal value: a vote in a marginal counts far more than a vote in a safe seat where the outcome is a foregone conclusion. **b** A reform to any other voting system, majoritarian or proportional, would enhance democracy. It would level the playing field in elections, and it would encourage voters to turn out if they felt two things: firstly that they had a choice and secondly that their vote registered and counted.

Other means of reforming the representative model could include the use of recall. **c** This would give an extra layer of accountability and control over MPs. Once elected, MPs now have virtual freedom until they go back to their constituency electors at the next election. Recall would give more power to the constituency voters, who may audit the work and input of their representative in an ongoing rather than summative fashion. This would make MPs take care in their work and prove themselves industrious and committed.

Representative democracy could be enhanced if the structures and institutions were to be updated. The continued existence of the House of Lords is an affront to any claim for democratic status: it is unelected and unaccountable. **d** Democracy would be enhanced if it were elected and its members subject to scrutiny. Accident of birth and prime-ministerial favour are not democratic qualifications to pass law. Other institutional changes could see power developed even more from Westminster to the regions and more political decisions made at a grassroots level.

A second way by which democracy could be enhanced is by the use of methods associated with direct democracy. **e** Three aspects can be considered. Firstly the greater use of referendums, secondly the introduction of initiatives, and finally greater consultation with the population. More referendums at all levels, both local and national, would improve democracy. They would enhance democracy and add a great deal of legitimacy to decisions. They would hold governments accountable at a national level and at a local level would be ideal to ensure that decisions met with local approval.

A second method is the development of initiatives; these are methods whereby the citizens can request a referendum to take place. Currently the government instigates a referendum via a parliamentary bill and as such it is the government who 'rations' the supply of referendums. However, if the citizens themselves could commence the process, democracy would be enhanced.

The greater involvement of citizens' in between elections would help. This could be via citizen juries or consultative focus groups/assemblies. These could really provide the continuous link between the government and the governed that is continually present in direct democracy. In addition the link could be built upon with the use of modern electronic technology, sometimes referred to as digital democracy. This ease of communication would allow instant feedback on new issues as they arose.

In conclusion, there are numerous methods by which democracy could be enhanced in the UK. It would be stretching the imagination if all these at one time would be considered and even implemented. What we see are gradual and incremental changes to the way in which democracy works. In the time of Labour, from 1997 to 2010, we saw referendums and devolution and some changes to the House of Lords. That is the nature of a mature and progressive democracy. We are likely to see constitutional reform to the House of Lords and some type of recall for errant MPs. Democracy is a 'work in progress' and will be added to and changed through time. **f**

⊙ **23/25 marks awarded:** 7/8 for AO1, 9/9 for AO2, 7/8 for AO3. Overall this response is well structured and keeps a close monitor throughout on the question. **a** There is a good introduction, which sets the scene and states the direction of travel. The response then provides a credible summary. **b** It looks at the electoral system and addresses both the how (AO1) and the why (AO2) aspect. In particular, it deals with specifics about the value of votes and uses good AO3 terminology to show comprehension. **c** Next it deals with a speculative issue, that of recall, and it does this in a credible fashion with the possible implications. **d** It then mentions structural reform and focuses on the House of Lords and makes the point 'why' linked to the question exceptionally well. More constitutional topics, such as a codified constitution or reform to the House of Commons, could have been chosen but in an exam we would not expect 100% coverage of every possible topic. **e** The answer then moves to introducing elements of direct democracy, covering initiatives, referendums and citizen participation. All this is done with a focus on both the method and the reasons supporting how democracy would be enhanced. **f** The conclusion is not extensive but it adds weight to the AO2 criteria and considers the long-term trends of how democracy in the UK has developed over time

Although, as noted above, more topics could have been advanced, for instance a compulsory voting or reducing the voting age, this is a strong A-grade answer: it develops the points well and keeps a focus throughout on the question.

Student B

There is a real need for democracy to be enhanced in the UK and there are several key ways by which this can be brought about.

Firstly there is a need for electoral reform to how MPs are elected to Westminster. We currently use first-past-the-post and this is unfair as no government in nearly 100 years has got 50% of the vote yet they claim 100% of the power. Electoral reform would make this system much fairer and we would get a government which reflects what the public voted for. **a** Many MPs themselves fail to get 50% of the vote in their constituencies. Electoral reform is crucial to improve turnout and expand participation levels. Turnout at elections has been falling and it is clear that the system is acting to 'disengage' people from politics. It would prevent the reliance of parties on huge numbers of safe seats and stop the election outcome being decided in just a few marginal seats, as these are the only ones which really matter in a general election. Sadly the public are ill informed of how the electoral system works and cannot see the huge benefit that electoral reform would deliver to them. However, there is an equally strong argument that implies we should keep the system for electing MPs as it is, for it is easy to understand and produces a very important link between an MP and their constituency. It also keeps extremist parties, who may harm democracy, out of being able to gain representation. **b**

We should also hold more referendums as these would be good as they are a link to direct democracy. We have only had two national ones and more referendums on moral issues such as euthanasia and abortion would be good and make people become more involved in current affairs. More referendums would solve areas where there is controversy and disagreement and make a decision final and binding so the country can move on. Equally there are views that referendums are no real help to improve politics as the public soon tire of them and issues cannot be condensed into a yes/no format. **c**

There is also a need to reform Parliament and make it more democratic. The recent expenses scandal showed how unfair the system was and in need of democratic reform. **d** The public would have more confidence if Parliament and MPs were better watched.

There are other ways by which democracy could be improved. Making people vote would increase turnout and get people more involved, and also using the internet and asking people their opinions would keep politicians in touch with what people wanted. **e**

There are clear ways by which democracy can be improved and action is urgently required.

ⓔ **13/25 marks awarded:** 5/8 for AO1, 4/9 for AO2, 4/8 for AO3. Electoral reform and the increased use of referendums get the best treatment in this response. **a** With electoral reform there is some good supporting evidence to develop the topic. Here we can see the use of both AO1 and AO2 in combination. **b** However, when the response moves to consider why the electoral system should not be reformed, there is limited reward as it moves away from the ambit of the question. **c** The section on referendums is not well expressed and could be developed to a higher level. **e** The weakness is then continued in the closing section and it is here that the response needs to be improved in the more speculative realm, in other words the 'how' is explained but not the 'why'. **d** The note of the expenses scandal is not hitting at the core issue of enhancing democracy, as this deals with personal financial gain as opposed to a systemic failure of democratic politics. This is a C-grade answer.

Question 2 **Party policies and ideas**

(a) Outline two political ideas associated with the term 'right wing'.   (5 marks)

ⓔ 'Left wing' and 'right wing' are two key terms on the specification. As a student of politics you should be able to define these and set out political ideas associated with them. Note that ideas differ from policies and this is at the core of the question; the policy is the practical development of the idea.

Student A

The political spectrum is often considered on a linear left-wing to right-wing divide with clear ideas defining each aspect. There are many political ideas which can be associated with the right wing in politics. One political idea is that where possible the role of the state in society should be reduced; this would allow business and enterprise maximum freedom. Similarly a reduced role for the state would encourage independence and prevent the development of a so-called 'dependency culture', which those on the right of the political spectrum feel is damaging. **a** A second idea associated with the right wing is to reduce wherever possible the levels of taxation and to ensure that companies and individuals can retain as much of their income as possible. **b** This is to encourage enterprise and not limit the rewards which success in business and personal life should reap.

ⓔ **5/5 marks awarded. a b** Here we see the full development of two political ideas associated with the right wing: a reduced role for the state and moves to reduce taxation levels. Each of these political ideas is developed by example and illustration to ensure that full marks are reached and an A grade awarded.

Student B

The term right wing is associated with the Conservative Party, all of their plans are considered to be right wing. **a** One example is law and order, which the Conservatives closely follow. They are keen to see people punished for crimes. This is to publicly demonstrate disapproval and deter others from turning to crime. **b** Secondly we can see that a right-wing idea is to bring back capital punishment or hanging for people who commit serious crimes such as murder, again the Conservatives believe that this would reduce crime levels. **c**

ⓔ **2/5 marks awarded. a** The opening comment is fine. **b** However, the main problem with this response is that it essentially covers only one idea and that is law and order. The second point which is raised, capital punishment, is really a development of the topic of law and order. **c** Furthermore, there is a lack of precision in the second point: right-wing policies may favour the use of capital punishment but it is not the official policy of the current Conservative Party. The answer just makes a grade C.

(b) Explain the nature of the divisions within the current Conservative Party. (10 marks)

ⓔ The Conservative Party like Labour has key divisions. These divisions contain different political ideas and subsequent policies.

Student A

All political parties to an extent are groups or factions united by common core principles and these groups or factions have a tendency to dominate through certain periods. The Conservative Party is no exception to this rule. **a** For the bulk of its history the one-nation section was the dominant force in the Conservative Party. This group can trace its origins back to Benjamin Disraeli in the 19th century and to the current Conservative prime minister, David Cameron, who in the run-up to the election stressed his one-nation credentials. There are several characteristics to one-nation conservatism. Firstly it stresses the need to avoid polar extremes in society between the rich and the poor: hence it stresses the duty inherent in the more affluent and wealthy to shoulder their stake in society. As such, this section sees the need for welfare and organisations such as the NHS. One-nation conservatism also is pragmatic and seeks to make changes in empathy with the existing structure, avoiding radical alternatives. Hence one-nation conservatives are likely to avoid constitutional changes unless absolutely necessary. One-nation conservatism also has paternalist characteristics, which seek to guide society, and searches for attempts to understand and not simply condemn. David Cameron's 'hug-a-hoodie' theme displayed these tendencies. **b**

Also within the current Conservative Party there is a strong faction which defines itself with the name derived from its leader from 1974 until 1990, Mrs Thatcher. These Conservative Party members are labelled as Thatcherites, and have a distinct set of beliefs, still compatible with the party. **c** Mrs Thatcher made a distinct difference to the party and created a distinct set of values in the party which pulled in different directions than the one-nation faction. Whereas as one-nation ideas stressed flexible pragmatism, Thatcherism was to stress radical alternatives, for instance in terms of the economy, where Thatcherism introduced privatisation. Where the one-nation group would advance paternalism, Thatcherism encouraged and promoted naked self-advancement. Hence abundant personal wealth was accepted and encouraged without the notion that the person who made this wealth had any moral duty to the society which allowed this advance. This gave rise to the saying associated with Thatcherism, 'There is no such thing as society'. In the 1980s the Thatcherite element grew in ascendancy in the party; the fall of Mrs Thatcher in 1990 dimmed but has not eradicated this section and today the party still shows both dimensions. **d**

ⓔ **10/10 marks awarded:** 7/7 for AO1, 3/3 for AO2. This is a very good A-grade response. **a** A brief one-line introduction notes the context of divisions within political parties. **b** The answer then moves straight into the nature of the one-nation section; the detail here is probably a little superfluous but the contemporary link with David Cameron is good. This shows how up to date the response is. **c** The second paragraph again exploits details on the nature of Thatcherism and draws on the ideas and the policies, which are developed. **d** The final comments could provide more detail about how the party is currently divided and how each faction of the party now positions itself.

Student B

The current Conservative Party has several splits inside its organisation. The main split is between the one-nation section and the Thatcherite group. **a** Mrs Thatcher successfully defeated the one-nation group in the 1980s as she won power from them and led the party with conviction politics. She built her power with victory in the Falklands over the Argentineans. In the UK Mrs Thatcher took on the trade unions and defeated their powers. For over 10 years the Conservative Party was led by Mrs Thatcher and she won three successive general election victories with considerable landslides. The main themes behind her policies were to praise and support businesses and give them as many advantages as possible to create wealth. At the same time she cut taxes so that people had more of their own money to spend and decide what to do with. This for many meant buying their own homes and she encouraged the selling of council houses. In companies she promoted the selling of state industries, and the public utilities such as gas, electricity and water were sold by the state to the private sector. Mrs Thatcher also made the Conservative Party turn against Europe and this caused some problems in the party. **b** However, when Mrs Thatcher left office, the party once again considered the one-nation section and encouraged consideration for poorer people who needed help in society.

🅔 **4/10 marks awarded:** 3/7 for AO1, 1/3 for AO2. **a** The answer opens well in defining the two key sections of the Conservative Party but then really only addresses in any detail half the question. Whereas there is a heavy emphasis on Mrs Thatcher, the one-nation section is mentioned but never developed or fully described. **b** The detail on Mrs Thatcher is relevant but it becomes more a personalised depiction than one that is fully based on policies and ideas. The answer receives a grade C.

(c) How and why do the major political parties differ over policies and ideas?   (25 marks)

🅔 Here the question asks for both policy and ideas. The 'how the parties differ' part of the question addresses AO1 (knowledge and understanding), the 'why' is the AO2 section. There is a need to constantly update your information to be competent in this area.

Student A

At election time and in front of the media the major political parties in the UK, the Conservatives and Labour, are keen to show their different ideas and how these move them to have a vastly differing set of policies between them. It is evident that they do stress and correctly point out their differences to voters in order to make them aware of how society would differ if their ideas are accepted and then their policies are put into place. **a**

It was quite clear in the run-up to the election and since that the Conservative Party had a clear difference over economic policy than Labour. They wished to make swifter cuts in public expenditure and took off an immediate £6 billion in public spending. They cut deeper and faster than Labour would have done (and also the Liberal Democrats, who echoed Labour's plans here in their manifesto). **b** Similarly in taxation policy, it is a Conservative idea to reduce taxes in order that people (and business) can retain as much of their income as possible. To secure this goal, national insurance was cut and also corporation tax. These policy ideas square with Conservative thinking that the role and scope of the state has to be reduced. **c**

Following up on this idea David Cameron was keen to extol the idea of the 'big society'. This is the idea that the role and scope of the state will be reduced and in its place individuals, groups and voluntary organisations will replace and fill the void. This can be seen to have links with ideas from one-nation and Thatcherite factions. **d** Encouraging individuals and organisations can be seen as integrating society and developing paternalist views; it may also be seen as a cloak to cover up what are essentially Thatcherite moves to cut the state. This preference and option for other agents than the state in public welfare as a coherent policy base is in contrast to the Labour Party who had no such role for this element in society.

The idea of rolling back the state continued in education where the Conservatives have created 'free schools', granting independence from the local authority in setting these up. Likewise the Conservatives aim to give existing state schools much more independence by fast-tracking academies and vastly increasing their number. In contrast Labour's ideas and policies were still to focus on quality improvements rather than major structural or strategic action.

As regards the EU, the Conservative Party have always had a strong Eurosceptic section and clearly stated in their manifesto that they would oppose joining the euro. The Labour Party was less opposed and promised a referendum before joining. To further distance themselves from Labour, the Conservatives outlined that no further powers would be granted to the EU unless Parliament approved of the action and ultimately the people in a referendum. The Labour Party was less hostile to the EU.

In respect of the electoral system used for Westminster MPs, the Conservatives were clear that they did not want a change to the system of first-past-the-post. They were willing to make constituencies more equal in size and reduce the number of MPs. In contrast the Labour Party was willing to hold a referendum on AV and consider change. Labour was not planning on reducing the number of MPs or vastly altering (or equalising) the number of constituents in certain seats. This move by the Conservatives is perhaps a pragmatic idea, the Labour Party does have an electoral benefit in the way in which the system currently operates and this move may eliminate that.

The Conservatives have been keen to dismantle what they did not like about the former government and to remove if possible traces of the ideas and polices of New Labour. One aspect of this is the idea to create a UK Bill of Rights to replace the ECHR-based version introduced by Labour. As part of the economic cutbacks, the Conservatives stopped a New Labour flagship policy which was the school building programme (Building Schools for the Future or BSF). Finally, the moves to introduce any form of ID card scheme was stopped in its tracks as David Cameron took up office. **e**

Although in manifesto terms there was no major difference between the parties as both promised a clear commitment to the NHS, the Conservatives planned to end target-setting goals such as waiting lists and league tables — again this being part of the previous Labour government's agenda. However, once in office, the Conservative plans for the NHS have been seen as far more radical and are accused of being disguised plans to privatise the service. Here the Labour Party is keen to state that these plans are completely opposite to their ideas and polices. **f**

In terms of the environment, the Conservative Party was keen to emphasise its difference from Labour. David Cameron set about developing these ideas in opposition, he wanted to portray the party as 'greener' than Labour. Part of this approach may be tied to the paternalistic one-nation view of showing care and concern for the good of the whole environment. In terms of policy, one sharp difference was that as soon as Labour left office David Cameron cancelled the building of the planned third runway at Heathrow, at the same time the plans for a high-speed rail link were advanced.

In conclusion it is clear to see differences between the major parties. Each has a distinct set of political ideas which generate differing policy options. However, at the same time all major parties are trying to win votes and support and as such their ideas may be diverted to ensure popularity as opposed to ideological purity. Furthermore it is equally possible to highlight a huge amount of policy options which are very similar. The latter gives credence that although the ideas may differ at source the policies do not, as the parties search to please the many and achieve power. **g**

@ **25/25 marks awarded:** 8/8 for AO1, 9/9 for AO2 and 8/8 for AO3. This is a complete and detailed answer packed with clearly expressed ideas and policy options, worthy of a top grade A. **a** A clear introduction outlines the scope of the response. **b** The reference to the Liberal Democrats is good; they have to be considered a major party as they now share government. **c** The link of idea and policy with reference to the Conservative Party is good here. **d** Indeed the theme continues with how David Cameron's ideas surrounding the 'big society' can be considered — this is an excellent example of AO2 marks. **e** The eradication of all things 'New Labour' is again good reflective work and merits reward in the AO2 category. **f** It is good to note more recent changes as parties take up the role of government. Prior to the election in 2010 the Conservatives stressed their staunch protection for the NHS but in government their plans have attracted more detailed questioning. **g** A neat conclusion summarises the response and considers the populist nature of political parties.

Student B

There are some who say that there is very little difference between the major political parties in the UK as their policies are so similar, however others stress that significant policy divides separate Labour and the Conservative Party.

If we looked at topic areas we can see that a wide division exists and we can trace this back to the party manifestos each party produced in the run-up to the May 2010 election. **a**

In the economy the Conservatives were keen to cut as quickly as they could and as they took office they made £6 billion of cuts in public spending. They were keen to reduce our debt as fast as they could. By contrast the Labour Party would not have cut spending and would have kept on borrowing, putting us more in debt. This shows that the Conservatives are more responsible and want to balance the books. The Labour Party would be frightened of cutting public spending as it would hurt the people who support the party and could spell trouble for them at the next election.

b The Labour Party was keen on joining the euro but the Conservatives were set against this policy and ruled it out. On taxes the Conservatives would like to reduce taxation and they have not introduced a rise in national insurance but the Labour Party was keen to tax as they introduced a top rate of 50p in the £ for high earners. The Conservatives have developed plans to reduce benefits for the higher earners also.

The Conservatives were less keen on changing the constitution and would keep things as they are but they would abolish the Human Rights Act as it comes from Europe — which the Conservatives oppose — and instead make a UK-only Bill of Rights such as they have in the USA. By contrast, as noted, the Labour Party is much keener on the EU. c

As for when people become 16, the Conservatives presented the plan to introduce a form of national service which meant joining the army, whereas for 16-year-olds Labour promised to consider allowing the vote for this age group. This hints that the Labour Party could be considered to be more democratic than the Conservatives on this area. d

In regards to the NHS the parties really differ. The Labour Party if in office would have continued to develop Foundation Hospitals, however the Conservatives have made major plans to really change how the NHS operates and some suggest that this is a form of privatising the service which Labour are set against.

In education the Conservatives are keen on academies and are creating free schools with more independence and less control from local authorities. The Conservatives have increased the fees for students who wish to go to university but the Labour Party is against fees. e

The Conservatives are more environmentally friendly and have stopped the third runway at Heathrow which Labour planned to develop. Labour was not as 'green' as the Conservatives who were more active in this area. f

ⓔ 13/25 marks awarded: 4/8 for AO1, 5/9 for AO2 and 4/8 for AO3. A mixed response, worthy of a grade C, this includes some clear comment but in other areas the material is inaccurate. a The last manifesto is a good starting point but care needs to be taken as many ideas can be traced back before 2010 and many key differences emerge once one a party takes up government. b In terms of the budget reduction, the detail on Labour is not clear. Labour had no plans to increase borrowing, and the comment about fear of cutting is not fully accurate. c The plan to create a UK-based Bill of Rights is correct but there is an implication that the current Human Rights Act comes from the EU when in fact it emanated from the ECHR. d The conclusion that the Labour Party is more democratic than the Conservative Party is hard to establish on this limited evidence. e f The last two points made are again not precise. First, it was Labour which introduced tuition fees and next, although it is accurate that the Conservative-led coalition abandoned plans for the third runway at Heathrow, both parties had similar detail on environmental issues at the 2010 election.

Question 3 Elections

(a) Outline two functions of elections.

(5 marks)

ⓔ This is a straightforward question. The important thing to note is that the term 'functions' indicates that the question is asking for the purposes that are served — put another way, what purposes do elections serve? Furthermore, the question is asking for positive functions and is not seeking evaluation or criticism of elections.

Student A

Elections serve many functions in a modern representative democracy. Firstly they serve to provide representation for citizens. This can be at a local level in a parliamentary constituency, and on a larger scale at European level to provide MEPs. A geographical area has a representative to speak and act on the people's behalf in national and European bodies. Secondly, elections provide a function of accountability when they serve to hold the current incumbents to account. This incumbent can be an MP or it may be the government as a whole. The function here of the election is to reflect the mood of the voters to either renew the term of office or replace those in post.

ⓔ **5/5 marks awarded.** A full grade-A answer. Two functions are depicted and the examples develop clarity and precision.

Student B

Elections are a very important part of our democracy and they are required to be held to prove our democratic status. In the UK we have elections for our prime minister and that gives us the ability to ensure that he is democratically elected. **a**

Secondly elections allow people to participate in democracy. We are not a direct democracy so elections have a function to allow everybody to participate and so at the end when all the counting is done it is fair as we all participate to see who has won fair and square. **b**

ⓔ **2/5 marks awarded.** This is a relatively weak answer, and receives a grade C. Two functions are noted but they are not expressed clearly. **a** The first point about democracy can be developed but the example of the prime minister is not really a good vehicle to deliver clarity. It would be preferable to develop the point about majoritarianism. **b** Likewise the second point about participation is a correct function but again it is poorly supported by example and is a little misleading as everyone has the option to participate but we do not get 100% turnout.

(b) Identify three advantages of proportional representation.

(10 marks)

ⓔ Here again the question is direct. The only note of caution is that the key element is the wider principles and concepts associated with proportional representation. It is relevant to consider proportional voting systems such as STV, the regional list etc. but that is not the precise nature of the question.

Proportional representation is the key principle whereby votes and seats are accurately correlated; hence if a party/candidate gets 25% of the vote they are rewarded with 25% of the seats. The reward in terms of seats is accurately reflected in the percentage of vote received. This is the first and most clear advantage of proportional representation: parties and candidates are fairly and accurately represented. There is no 'winner's bonus' whereby a party with a minimal lead has an exaggerated winning margin. Quite simply the vote collected is accurately converted into a fair and corresponding share of the seats. **a**

A second advantage of proportional representation is that all votes are of equal value no matter where they are cast. It truly delivers the theme that one vote has one value. Proportional representation aims to ensure that any constituency or geographical bias is eliminated. Safe seats would not exist if a system of proportional representation were to be used. **b**

Building on from the above point delivers a third advantage of proportional representation: better representation. Small parties which are unable to convert their votes into seats under other less accurate methods can see their political influence increase. Parties which fail under systems such as first-past-the-post are given political life and a voice in the political system which they are due. It could also be linked to encouraging voters in all and every constituency or area to vote as they know that their vote for a smaller party will not be wasted. Indeed that last point concerning wasted votes is a key advantage often claimed to be eliminated under proportional representation. **c** Achieving proportional representation can be delivered by a huge range of voting or electoral systems, and the debate as to the best type of system and their features is another contested topic.

ⓔ **9/10 marks awarded:** 6/7 for AO1, 3/3 for AO2. **a** The response begins well, defining the term and in so doing explaining a prominent advantage claimed for proportional representation. **b** The second advantage again sets out the principle of the equal value of votes; the example supporting this could be developed further but the point is clear. **c** The third advantage is better detailed and it explains how the fortunes of smaller parties can be enhanced if proportional representation were to be used. Time is limited in a part (b) question but reference could be made to the advantages which would arise in the UK if the Westminster system for electing MPs were to be changed, though it is not essential. This answer would achieve an A grade.

Proportional representation has many advantages but it does have some drawbacks. It has been used in the devolved assemblies and is widely used in the rest of Europe. If so many people can use it all over Europe then why can it not be used more widely in the UK? If it was it would make our MPs more fairly elected. **a**

The first advantage is that proportional representation works out what is fair at the outcome and the share of the vote is evened out and not piled up as in first-past-the-post elections. In first-past-the-post votes are wasted and this often deters people from voting as they know it will be worthless. This leads on to the second advantage that more people will vote under proportional representation than under first-past-the-post and if more people vote this will make the outcome clear and fair.

Currently the outcome of our elections can be unfair as candidates can win seats and they do not have 50% of the vote. Over two-thirds of MPs do not get 50% of the vote in their constituencies. A final advantage of proportional representation is that small parties are given a real chance of gaining representation which under other systems they cannot. This allows all sections of society to be given a voice and express their opinions. However, it can spell trouble as small parties can hold an unfair advantage over the larger parties. Overall, proportional representation brings many advantages and should replace first-past-the-post. **b**

ⓔ **4/10 marks awarded:** 3/7 for AO1, 1/3 for AO2. **a** Off to a strange start here as the drawbacks are not asked for in the question, indeed the first paragraph does not focus on the question and produces no marks. **b** The next paragraph is confused: several things may be inferred. The comment may refer to the fact that proportional representation may eradicate heartlands and electoral deserts where in certain seats voters may feel their vote is wasted. It will gain some credit but the point is far from clear. In a similar vein, the second point about increased turnout is supposition, with no evidence presented. The supplementary point about the current system is again tangential as it seeks to criticise an existing system as opposed to defining clearly an advantage of proportional representation. The final advantage is clear; however, once again, time and focus are lost as the response still seeks to develop disadvantages with proportional representation and this is not the question! The response fails to get off the ground and it is thwarted by making erroneous comments. It would receive a grade C.

(c) Make out a case in favour of retaining the system of first-past-the-post used for Westminster elections.
(25 marks)

ⓔ Once again, this is a clearly defined question. Take note that here the request is to make a case on *one side* of a contested debate — electoral reform — and to defend the system of first-past-the-post. The AO2 component will be extracted among other things from how well the assessment of the strengths of the current system is completed. Answers to questions such as this will be expected to make some reference to failings but to come to a view that these criticisms are unsound. The question does ask you to stand on one side of the fence. In this respect it differs from questions which are phrased 'To what extent...', as these call for you to examine *both* sides and to come to an independent position in conclusion.

Student A

There have been many calls for the removal of the system of first-past-the-post used to elect MPs to Westminster. However, the resilience and preference for the current system remains in place. The outcome of the referendum on 5 May 2011 has to a large extent added a considerable public voice illustrating the lack of desire to change the current voting system used to elect our MPs to Westminster. Supporters of first-past-the-post claim the advantages of the system far outweigh any disadvantages and thus the case in favour is strong and clear. **a**

First-past-the-post is a simple plurality electoral system. In order to secure victory in a constituency a candidate has to gain a minimum of a one vote advantage over their nearest rival. The larger the margin, from one vote to thousands, the outcome is the same victory in that seat. The percentage which the winning candidate gains will often not account for 50% of the vote but a winning margin as small as one is all that is required. The winning post as such in a constituency is determined when all the votes are counted. In addition each constituency only returns one candidate. At a national level to win the general election (and be able to form a government alone) a party must win half of the 650 seats +1, which is 326. In this sense there is a pre-determined finishing post. The above facts serve to illustrate the transparent nature of first-past-the-post and a reason for its retention. Using other systems the calculation has to take place after the vote and possibly some redistribution of votes. With first-past-the-post there is no such post-election calculation. **b**

Moreover the system has to be favoured for its simplicity and ease of use. All that is required is for the voter to place an 'X' by their choice. There is no need to rank candidates or to make more than one preference — in contrast to other more complicated systems where confusion arises. For example, there are a huge number of spoilt papers under various types of PR as a result of voter confusion. In Scotland when STV was used there were thousands of spoilt ballot papers. **c** This is evidence that citizens are denied democracy. The case for retaining FPTP is thus bolstered.

Speed is another lauded attribute of first-past-the-post and a reason for its retention. We often get the results in constituencies just hours after the polls close and the verdict on who will secure the ability to govern alone before the next dawn breaks. A new prime minister can be entering number 10 at lunchtime the following day. By contrast other electoral systems can take days to calculate as votes are redistributed. In the Republic of Ireland it can take many days to discover who has the ability to form a government as recounts and redistributions continue under the system of STV. **d**

Building on this with very few exceptions the current system delivers clear results with one party being able to govern alone. The government which emerges invariably has a clear working majority and this means that it can pass legislation and carry out without difficult operative restrictions the task of government. The system avoids coalitions where deals have to be made after the election rather than before and government may take some time to form. There is more chance of a coalition being weak than a single-party government being weak. It is not uncommon for problems to arise in coalition agreements and we can see this in the coalition partnership between the Liberal Democrats and the Conservatives. Hence strength and stability often linked together are claimed attributes for first-past-the-post. **e**

Furthermore first-past-the-post has a clear sense of accountability running through it. It serves to make a clear choice in terms of party to govern. It also serves to make a clear statement of disapproval by throwing out a government. **f** All too often minor parties can remain in office as they switch major partner under alternative systems to first-past-the-post. A good example of this is in post-war Germany where major parties may differ but the centrist party remained in power. Thus first-past-the-post denies providing major power to minor parties. Again here is evidence to support its retention.

Finally first-past-the-post retains and nurtures an MP–constituency link. Each area in the UK can claim to have a representative in the House of Commons with whom they can identify and who can act in the best interests of their locality. This loyalty cuts across political party boundaries, and representatives work on behalf of all the community, not just those who voted for them. This system serves to ensure representative democracy works, for it connects elected politicians with the public who elect them.

In conclusion there are numerous arguments which support first-past-the-post. It may have some defects but they are vastly outweighed with the above advantages. Furthermore, as noted at the outset, the public demand for reform does not exist as the referendum verdict displayed and reform is now less likely than ever. First-past-the-post still has a long time to run. **g**

e **24/25 marks awarded:** 8/8 for AO1, 8/9 for AO2 and 8/8 for AO3. **a** A clear introduction focuses on the question and adds insight with latest developments. **b** Here the response sets out how first-past-the-post operates and this allows for the advantages to be drawn out later in the paragraph. It is good to see candidates understand the mechanics of the simple plurality system. **c** Although the response does not differentiate majoritarian systems from full systems of proportional representation, the idea of ranking candidates is important and again a good example supports the point, linking AO1 and AO2 together. **d** Here a similarly-styled point is made and done well: clarity in detail supplemented by an example. **e** The oft-made claim for strength and stability is shown. The example could be enhanced — for instance, it could give the example of the Thatcher or Blair governments being able to implement their radical agendas. **f** In recent times the 1997 election was seen as an election where the public disapproved of the incumbent government, severely punishing the Conservative Party as it only collected 166 seats. **g** The conclusion looks back to the question and provides the themes of consistency and continuity. This is a top level 3 response, well into the terrain of a grade A.

Student B

First-past-the-post is so simple and easy to use and all electors know how to vote as it only involves placing a cross next to your choice. Other systems which rank candidates can be seen as complicated and misleading. Alternative systems mean that people who do not win outright on the first calculation come to win after time, and to many voters this seems unfair; to some it seems like the winner of the race is put behind and it does not seem right. **a**

Next is the time factor, counting crosses is quicker than calculating preferences or redistributing seats in any way. In some countries working out who has won takes days and the precision and sharpness of first-past-the-post is to be admired. **b**

So it is traditional to use first-past-the-post and people do not like to break tradition as we have seen in the result of the referendum. People wanted to keep with what they knew so there is no support for change to proportional representation. We use other systems in the devolved regions and these are complicated and the public do not like them and they produce governments which fail and do not work. Italy is known to be an unstable and unsafe country and that is because it does not use first-past-the-post, but strong countries like the UK and the USA do and this makes them powerful. **c**

Two parties are all that is needed in a political system; having more gives too much choice and if a party does not get many votes it should not have a say in how we run our country. With lots of small parties you get coalitions and they are bad.

First-past-the-post stops coalitions normally, it is rare that we had this happen in May 2010 and is unlikely to happen again as now the Liberal Democrats are so unpopular. It will be between two parties next time and this is much better for democracy. **d**

Keeping our current system means we know who to blame and can get rid of them really easily at the next election as we can vote them out, but other systems mean that you can never really get rid of governments as some parties always win and keep in post. **e**

Finally, under other systems you may never really know who your MP is as the party could decide this for you as they put them on lists which voters cannot see. This makes them favourites of the party not of the people and this is not democratic. **f**

Thankfully the referendum has finally put a stop to changes and first-past-the-post will be with us for the future as it has such strong support. **g**

ⓔ **10/25 marks awarded;** 4/8 for AO1, 3/9 for AO2 and 3/8 for AO3. **a** The answer begins without any form of introduction or consideration of the question asked. Also the point raised is correct but not well expressed. **b** It then continues briefly but concisely. An example would help here. It would be possible to show the normal swiftness of the current system, with May 2010 being the exception, or the weeks it took to form a government in Germany at its last national election. **c** The point concerning tradition is correct, but a better response would give some facts about the 2011 referendum. Furthermore, the example is flawed here — there is no clamour to remove the electoral system in the devolved areas and the conclusion inferred is incorrect. This would not lose marks but it does not gain them. The point concerning Italy and then the UK and USA is not really accurate; it requires further development. **d** Next we have several points running into one another and the impact of this convolution is damaging. It is better to keep points single and focused. The first point that is implied is that first-past-the-post keeps us with two parties. This is not really true. Perhaps the electoral system works better with just two in contention but if first-past-the-post was to be seen to deny choice this would be undemocratic. Democracy needs a range of parties. The negative aspects of coalitions could be developed much better than simply a speculation about the Conservative–Liberal Democrat coalition. This may be true but it needs more precision. Italian governments have a record of instability and the UK and US have governments which serve longer terms, but it is stretching the point too far to imply that Italy is 'unsafe' and what makes the UK and USA safe is first-past-the-post. **e** This paragraph contains a relevant point. **f** Here the use of an example would lift the response. It would be possible to cite the closed party list system used to elect MEPs. It needs to say that possibly in multi-member constituencies the close relationship is lost. Secondly, it is the senior party members who place candidates in rank order. Voters have to accept the party's rank order of candidates. Once again the point is not well expressed and explained. This means that the AO3 component is damaged in the process. It deals with accountability (a point which could be linked to coalitions) and this is a key attribute claimed for first-past-the-post. **g** The final paragraph is not a strong conclusion. It does not draw together the points in the response and is itself brief and undeveloped. Overall, this merits a grade C.

Question 4 **Pressure groups**

(a) Define, using examples, two differences between an insider and an outsider pressure group.   (5 marks)

ⓔ There are only two types of classification required by the specification. It is vital that you thoroughly master these key terms and prepare and revise clear examples. Detail and descriptive elements concerning pressure groups will not be lost in this area.

Student A

Insider and outsider pressure groups were defined by Wyn Grant. They relate to how close and productive a working relationship exists between pressure groups and the government. One difference is that an insider pressure group will have a close working relationship with government ministers and the civil service. For example, the National Farmers' Union has close links with DEFRA, but other groups such as the outsider Animal Liberation Front (ALF) have no such contact. **a**

A second difference is that it is more likely that outsider groups are more prone to turn to direct action than insider groups. Hence the outside group Fathers4Justice often carried out illegal stunts on public buildings, whereas insider groups such as the Confederation of British Industry (CBI) would use channels and openings to contact the government. **b**

ⓔ **5/5 marks awarded.** Full marks: this is an A-grade response. **a** A brief definition sets the scene and a clear working example is given as requested. **b** This is followed by a second clear definition showing a difference between the two types of pressure group. It notes that direct action is less likely from insiders but does not totally rule it out. The examples cited are correct.

Student B

Insider and outsider groups are completely different and can be easily set apart from each other. Firstly insider groups will have contact with the prime minister and all the government, but outsiders will not be allowed this chance as they are extreme. So the British Medical Association will see the government but the Animal Liberation Front will not be allowed to do so. **a**

A second difference is that outsiders will use violence and break the law but insiders will always abide by the law as they have government contact. An example of this is the Association of Chief Police Officers (ACPO) who definitely will not break the law and the IRA who use bombs and killings to secure their aims. **b**

ⓔ **3/5 marks awarded.** This answer is on the right lines but there is a need to be 'spot on' to ensure full marks. **a** The examples of insider and outsider are correct but the detail on contact is not precise. **b** The second difference is again weak. It makes a general statement which is not necessarily true: not all outsiders use violence. The use of the IRA as an example of an outsider group is not accurate. The IRA has to be considered to be a terrorist group rather than a pressure group. Given that there are so many examples of outsiders, this should be avoided. The answer just about gets 3 marks and a grade C, but with care and attention to detail it is so easy to gain full marks on these short questions.

(b) Identify three reasons why pressure groups fail to attain their goals. (10 marks)

ⓔ Quite often a part (b) question will contain the numerical request of 'three'. It is expected that three points in the 10 minutes available can be explained and exampled. You should always aim to meet these two criteria.

Student A

Success and failure are often on a knife edge for many pressure groups. There is a tendency only to detail the success, but in terms of outcomes failure tends to dominate in results but not in recollection. **a**

One of the main things which determine if a pressure group fails is if it cannot get a broad section of public opinion on its side to make the government listen. Currently a range of pressure groups such as Exit International and Dying in Dignity have all failed. A critical mass of the general public plus a fear of various governments has meant their campaign to change the law has failed. **b**

If a new government takes office with very set policies and principles, it may mean that some pressure groups face inevitable failure. The Stop the War campaign, which began in 2001, failed to stop a determined government under Blair to send in troops to Afghanistan and Iraq. Likewise a broad range of trade unions has not prevented the coalition government from the cuts it has announced in public services. Even the best-organised and well-financed pressure groups will fail if a determined government opposes their claims. **c**

Pressure groups may fail as a consequence of employing the wrong tactics. There may be negative press for certain actions. For example if certain unions go on strike and it causes hardship for innocent victims this can backfire against the union. Striking British Airways cabin crew have angered passengers as they have had holiday arrangements cancelled. The direct action of groups such as Fathers4Justice did not endear commuters to their cause as they held up traffic. The actions of the Animal Liberation Front, in releasing mink in Hampshire, were described as a 'disaster' for their cause. Their actions brought about a serious environmental disaster for the area. It set the wider campaign back as it brought disunity and bad press on all anti-fur groups. **d** It is inevitable that the majority of pressure groups will fail, there is only enough money and enough time for the minority to succeed. However, that success inspires so many more to continue in their respective pursuits.

ⓔ **10/10 marks awarded:** 7/7 for AO1, 3/3 for AO2. **a** There is no need for an introduction but this opening paragraph is precise and guides the response well on its way. It should perhaps include a brief explanation of what 'success' may mean. **b** A good example is used to illustrate a vital point, that of getting a critical mass following which a government has to listen to. **c** Governments will ignore pressure groups if they do not necessarily benefit the government's wider self-interest. A determined pressure group will often stand up to the government. Other examples, a little more dated, would include the Thatcher government's stance against trade unions in the 1980s. **d** The issue of tactics is used well. There could be a tendency to imply that all direct action is a failure and that would be incorrect. The examples cited define the context well. This question was done really well, the points are fully explained and the examples selected perfectly support the points raised. Well worth a grade A.

There can be many reasons why pressure groups do not achieve their aims. You have to have money for this is crucial to get success. Pressure groups that have money have a huge increase in chances as they can hire staff and premises to get their message across to others. Success has come to pressure groups such as the WWF and Greenpeace as they have vast financial reserves and can advertise and get consultants. If a pressure group has not got money it is very limited and doomed to fail. **a**

Next having a celebrity is a real positive for a pressure group; it is almost as if it gets free advertisement from a high-profile member. The Ghurkha Justice Campaign benefited enormously from the endorsement and membership of Joanna Lumley; similarly the support of people such as Jamie Oliver brings success for pressure groups. It becomes quite obvious for some pressure groups that if you cannot attract a celebrity to endorse or become involved the pressure group will fail. **b**

Finally pressure groups' success depends on insider or outsider status. An insider pressure group will almost certainly reach its aims and objectives and an outsider will fail. The British Medical Association (BMA), as it is an insider group, always obtains what it requires from government; similarly trade unions and business groups as known insiders are nearly certain that the government will be sympathetic. Outsiders such as Earth First! or Plane Stupid have literally no chance of success as they are real outsiders. **c**

⊜ **4/10 marks awarded:** 3/7 for AO1, 1/3 for AO2. **a** The response begins well but it provides evidence for success in more depth than it provides detail on reasons for failure; the case rests on 'you need this for success and if you have not got it then you fail'. Some credit can be gained but this is the wrong approach. **b** The same approach continues in the second paragraph, where success is again more clearly outlined than is failure. We have no illustration of a pressure group failing through lack of celebrity backing. **c** The theme of reverse information is complete. There is a little inconsistency in the final paragraph. It is quite possible that insiders (which vastly outnumber outsiders) will fail. The BMA has not been able to persuade the current government to scrap its plans for the NHS. Similarly, the government has given in to several outsider groups over the years such as the Ghurkhas as noted above and The League Against Cruel Sports, seen as an outsider, did achieve its goals. This response falters through a lack of care; the question has not been fully adhered to and the easier option of success is targeted by default. A C-grade answer.

(c) Do pressure groups distribute or restrict power in the political system?

(25 marks)

⊜ Half of the key terms on the specification relate to power and its distribution. The concepts of pluralism, elitism and pluralist democracy are crucial to successfully handling pressure group questions. The nature of the debate that needs to be addressed is set out by the way in which the question is worded.

Pressure groups are a significant force in a representative democracy such as the UK. Indeed it may be suggested that their importance has grown so much that political life would be problematic and even impossible without them. The focus, however, is on whether pressure groups act to distribute power or whether they operate in a restrictive manner and create a possible imbalance. Essentially, do pressure groups fit within a pluralist concept of power or, by contrast, if pressure groups function within an elitist version of power, can this be seen as restrictive? **a**

There is evidence that pressure groups distribute political power and adhere to pluralist theory. At its core, pluralism states that power and influence are very broadly and evenly distributed in political life and society. All have equal and fair access to make their views known and felt. There are no restrictions on stating a political case or viewpoint. The political world is evenly balanced with numerous and competing groups. No pressure group by itself or a small number of groups hold vast amounts of power to make political life unbalanced and uneven, almost as if it were an unfair contest: elitism does not apply. This gives rise to the belief that we have a pluralist democracy. **b**

Evidence that power is distributed can be seen by the fact that citizens are well represented through being a member of one if not several pressure groups. These pressure groups speak up for them on several fronts. Hence an individual may have an economic interest group working for them in relation to their occupation such as a trade union, they may be a member of a promotional group such as the RSPB. It is clear from the vast number of pressure groups and their equally vast membership that power is being dispersed. The RSPB has more members than all the political parties represented in all institutions in the UK, trade unions have nearly 9 million members, with hundreds of thousands in various environmental and animal welfare groups, and the list could go on. Power is dispersed as it is invested by the public in a multitude of groups.

Next it has to be considered if these groups have relevant political influence. For if they are simply groups with no power then the claim for pluralism and power dispersal is weak. Power for each group has to be considered as relative to its cause. Again evidence would appear to support this. Pressure groups have the ability to influence the general public, other sections of society and government and the political institutions. Hence local groups campaigning at a local level will be heard just as large national groups can leave their mark. Greenpeace is listened to by governments and others and the local media is full of examples where pressure groups act to influence change, for example in rural areas school closure programmes have had in-depth focus and attention.

Resources are fully available to all groups so that they can be politically active. Here the advance of the internet and mobile phone technology means that pressure groups have the ability to promote their message and at the same time spread their influence and power. **c**

Finally one key component of pluralism is that no group or set of groups dominate. This arises because each pressure group will most likely have its opposition to dampen and challenge. This again can be considered accurate, trade unions are faced with employer groups such as the CBI, pro-hunting groups such as the Countryside Alliance are faced with the League Against Cruel Sports, Pro-Life groups compete with Pro-Choice groups.

In summary, certainly some pressure groups will enjoy greater success but the political arena is open to all pressure groups and the process is accessible for all. The factors behind that success will vary and are not predictable in each case.

However, there is an opposing view that pressure groups restrict power in the political system and they are better defined by reference to elite theory. Elite theory implies that we see a concentration of political power with a minority of pressure groups exercising that power. **d**

The notion that citizens are well represented through membership of pressure groups is said to be incorrect. Membership may be high but this membership is not used for political activity, it is passive and inactive. It has been characterised as passive and labelled as 'cheque book membership'. This is compounded by the fact that these pressure groups lack any formal democratic credentials and serve a narrow interest of the internal hierarchy.

Building on from this it is alleged by elite theory that the levels of political influence of pressure groups vary tremendously. Some groups as a result of their wealth and status carry such great power that smaller less wealthy pressure groups stand no chance of exerting any influence or power. An example would be rich business groups which have a dominant position with all governments; in contrast trade unions or consumer groups stand little chance of success against these groups. This may be considered to be power of 'core insider' groups which have a really close and influential grip over government. The grip may be so well exerted that the general public may not be aware of its scope and impact as they work so well behind the scenes. This action would dispel the notion that pressure groups distribute power: they covertly concentrate it.

The theory of elite concentration of power was developed by C.W. Mills in his work *The Power Elite*, elite theory having before been raised by other political scientists such as Michels and Mosca. At its core it argues that powerful pressure groups simply continue to dominate and the notion of a plural and open political forum for alternative pressure group power is nonsense.

In conclusion, there are two clear positions; do pressure groups distribute power and this is supported by pluralism, or do pressure groups restrict the flow of power and are characterised by elitism. On the surface, elitism has more evidence in its favour. Success tends to flow to the groups with money, expertise and existing connections. The notion of universal membership of the pressure group world is misleading: many are outside the process and denied any real influence or power. We see occasional success for some pressure groups which manage to capture enough public support to succeed but in the background the wealthy and established pressure groups show that power is restricted.

ⓔ 25/25 marks awarded: 8/8 for AO1, 9/9 for AO2 and 8/8 for AO3. **a** This begins with a really good introduction. The key concepts of elitism and pluralism are noted and explained; this is at the core of the question. **b** The detail linking pluralism and pluralist democracy shows excellent comprehension of the topic. **c** Possibly the response more could be developed with regard to resources. **d** The response shows balance, noting alternative theory and later making reference to elite theorists. It ends with a clear conclusion and one in which the question raised is focused upon and an answer provided. It would be equally acceptable had the response decided to support pluralist theory as long as evidence is provided to support the position. An excellent A-grade answer — it constantly keeps the question in mind. The case for pluralism receives perhaps more coverage, but even if there are two positions to adopt it is not always vital to spend exactly equal time on each, as long as each contested viewpoint is covered.

Student B

Pressure groups are a key part of the UK's political system and they bring tremendous benefits for society. They have grown rapidly since 1945 and also since the advance of the internet it is now easy to find pressure groups that can help a person in any walk of life and with any problem. **a**

To show that they distribute power we need to look at the vast range in existence, and see that there are groups for and against topics. **b** Good examples are the groups for and against foxhunting. There are anti-hunting groups who wish to prevent blood sports and pro-hunting groups such as the Countryside Alliance.

Pressure groups also distribute power as they provide representation which would not otherwise be provided. They allow minority groups to have a political voice, a voice which political parties are not able to provide. This spreads power and also influence. For instance, in between elections, pressure groups can wield power by asking governments to act and answer key issues. They spread power as they educate the general public and inform and alarm them. For instance, pressure groups tell the public of the danger to the environment. Greenpeace has long warned of the dangers to the ozone layer and to species eradication.

In some respects pressure groups distribute power as they provide expertise and specialist knowledge to government. For instance, in certain areas the government requires informed groups to provide information. The government works and needs the National Farmers' Union (NFU) if it is to make changes to agricultural policy.

Finally pressure groups can check government and ensure that it acts fairly and openly. Pressure groups, by watching policy and voicing opinion, are good for democracy and this is helped by a free press. **c**

However, pressure groups can restrict power in the political system. They do this by not being accountable as they can have enormous power and no responsibility. The trade unions in the 1970s were accused of this by the Conservative Party and so Mrs Thatcher cut back on their influence.

Pressure groups are inherently selfish and this is especially true of sectional groups which have no concern if their aims and agendas are socially and politically divisive. This can cause trouble in society.

The most dangerous aspect which they promote is that they undermine democracy and take away Parliament's power and the power of elected representatives. It is as though they have a disproportionate amount of power for their narrow interest which they advance. **d**

So, in conclusion, we can see that there are good and bad aspects to pressure groups and they do move power around. The extent of that movement depends on a lot of factors. The barriers preventing success will hold the power of pressure groups back.

e **10/25 marks awarded:** 4/8 for AO1, 3/9 for AO2 and 3/8 for AO3. **a** We begin with an odd introduction; it is very general and is not focused on the question. **b** The question is then addressed but it is still not clear and detailed. **c** As the response is more focused on the good things which pressure groups do in a democratic society, it is as if the question is being avoided.

The concept of pluralism and pluralist democracy, which is at the core of this question, has not been developed and as such this is going to limit the reward available. **d** Three points are made as indication for the restriction of power but there is no focus on elitism and narrow sectional interest. This part of the response reads more as an account of how pressure groups damage democracy and as such it is not directly collecting marks. Also, only three brief points are discussed. Overall this answer would merit a grade C.

Knowledge check answers

This section gives you summaries of the answers to the knowledge checks contained in each topic. You can see how accurately and comprehensively you were able to answer the questions.

1
- The monarchy is legitimate because it has traditional authority and, though not elected, it is widely accepted that it has a right to provide the head of state as long as the monarch plays no political role.
- The House of Lords also claims traditional legitimacy. It also derives some legitimacy from the fact that most of its members have been appointed by elected, accountable politicians. Hereditary powers, however, can scarcely claim legitimacy.
- The House of Commons is far more legitimate as it is elected and is accountable.
- The prime minister has legitimacy because it is widely accepted that the leader of the winning party at an election should be prime minister. He or she is therefore indirectly elected. The PM obtains legitimacy from the electorate, his or her party and Parliament.

2
The *positive aspects* of direct democracy should include these key points:
- It is the purest form of democracy. Referendums demonstrate this.
- It is the will of the majority in a society. Again, referendums guarantee this, though, if the turnout is low, the result may be invalidated.
- People are more likely to consent to decisions they have made themselves or on which they were consulted. Thus the introduction of an elected mayor in London was accepted because it was the subject of a London referendum.

The *negative aspects* of direct democracy should include at least these three points:
- The will of the majority may represent the 'tyranny of the majority' and result in the oppression of minorities. This occurred in California in 2008 when an initiative resulted in the banning of civil partnerships. This was seen as discrimination against the gay community.
- People may become politically fatigued by voting too often. This was illustrated by the low turnout in the 2011 AV referendum, only 1 year after a general election.
- People may find some issues too complex to decide upon. This may have been one of the reasons for the low turnout and negative vote in the AV referendum.

3
The key distinctions are these:
- With direct democracy the people themselves make decisions. In representative democracy decisions are made by elected representatives.
- Direct democracy is the will of the majority, while representative systems can mediate between different minority groups.
- Representative systems can handle complex, technical issues. This is difficult with direct democracy.
- Direct democracy may result in emotional, irrational decisions. Representative democracies are more likely to result in rational decisions.

4
Important reasons are these:
- There have been more constitutional reforms and these need popular consent. The devolution referendums of 1997 were examples.

- Governments and politicians are less trusted than in the past, so referendums solve the problem. This was partly the case with the Northern Ireland referendum on the Good Friday Agreement in 1998.
- People are better informed. It was hoped that the issues surrounding the 2011 AV referendum could be understood by the electorate.
- Governments have discovered that referendums can solve internal splits. This was the case with the 1975 vote on British membership of the European Community.

5
Ways in which Britain is a liberal democracy include:
- There are regular free elections — usually every 4 or 5 years.
- Rights and freedoms are protected — the Human Rights Act.
- The rule of law applies — all are equal under the law.
- There is tolerance of many beliefs, cultures and ideas — freedom of expression, thought and worship are protected by law.

Ways in which Britain is *not* a liberal democracy include:
- There are unelected institutions — the House of Lords and the monarchy.
- Rights and freedoms can be threatened — Parliament remains sovereign and can ignore legal rights.
- There is no entrenched, codified constitution, so government is not limited.
- The electoral system for general elections is often considered unfair and undemocratic — the first-past-the-post electoral system.

6
Ways of increasing political participation include:
- votes at 16 plus — but young people may not understand the issues
- compulsory voting — but it forces the uninformed to vote and abuses the freedom not to vote
- more referendums — but people may suffer voter fatigue, people may lose respect for representative institutions, some issues may be too complex for the general population. Referendums may produce uninformed, irrational responses
- increasing use of the internet for consultation — but this may be misused by organised campaigns and may be affected by fraud
- citizenship education — but expensive and there is little evidence it will have an effect

7
Key distinctions between the political left and right include:
- The left supports collectivism. The right promotes individualism.
- The left supports social and economic action by the centralised state. The right is suspicious of state power.
- The left opposes inequality and promotes redistribution of income. The right accepts inequality as natural.
- The left sees welfare as a right for the poor and underprivileged. The right sees welfare as a last resort and a disincentive to work and enterprise.
- The left believes that key industries should be under state control or supervision. The right believes in free markets.
- The left supports trade unions as a means of protecting workers' interests. The right sees unions as a barrier to free markets and innovation.

8
Consensus issues include:
- the need to reduce government debt as rapidly as possible
- reduction of income tax for low earners
- strict targets on emissions reduction
- continued support for state education and health provision
- the need to reform the House of Lords, making it more democratic

Agreements to differ include:

- whether to develop nuclear energy further
- whether to renew Britain's Trident nuclear missile system
- taxation level for the very wealthy
- the need for electoral reform
- how far the NHS needs to be reformed

9 Ways in which New Labour differs from traditional Labour include these:

- New Labour accepted weak trade unions, whereas traditional Labour favoured strong trade unions.
- Traditional Labour brought large, key industries under state control, while New Labour opposed this and supported free markets and free enterprise.
- New Labour supported individualism, while traditional Labour is collectivist.
- Traditional Labour seeks to redistribute income from rich to poor to a much greater extent than New Labour.
- New Labour saw private home ownership as a key aspiration, while traditional Labour supported social housing for the less well off.

10 Differences between the Thatcherite New Right and traditional conservatism include these:

- The New Right sees society as a collection of individuals, while traditional conservatives see society as organic.
- The New Right is dogmatic in its beliefs, while traditional conservatives are pragmatic.
- Traditional conservatives are more supportive of traditional institutions than the New Right.
- Traditional conservatives are more supportive of state welfare systems than the New Right, which opposes a 'dependency culture'.
- The New Right opposes excessive state control of the economy, while traditional conservatives tolerate a good deal of state control.

11 Ways in which Liberal Democrat policies conform to traditional liberalism include these:

- the belief in stronger constitutional protection of rights and liberties
- support for an entrenched, codified constitution
- tolerance of different beliefs and cultures
- strong support for measures to increase equality of opportunity
- greater tolerance of criminal behaviour, seeing it largely as the result of social deprivation
- support for social justice measures, including some redistribution of income from rich to poor

12 The principles of manifesto and mandate were challenged by coalition government in these ways:

- The coalition agreement was a combination of two manifestos. Thus many manifesto commitments were abandoned by both parties.
- Because there was no single manifesto for the coalition, it cannot claim a genuine electoral mandate.
- Some policies were adopted which were in neither manifesto and thus had no mandate. NHS reform is an example.

13 *Effective* aspects of first-past-the-post include:

- It usually delivers strong, single-party government with a majority in the House of Commons.
- It establishes a strong relationship between MPs and constituencies.

- It is easy to understand and the negative referendum vote on AV in 2011 suggests it enjoys widespread support.

Ineffective aspects of first-past-the-post include:

- It produces governments with a minority of the popular vote, thus lacking legitimacy.
- It distorts the level of support for parties, especially small ones which are discriminated against.
- Many MPs are elected on a minority vote.
- Many votes are in effect wasted.
- Votes are of unequal value.
- It forces many people to vote tactically.

14 Reasons for introducing proportional representation for general elections include these:

- The membership of Parliament will more accurately reflect support for all parties.
- It will help small parties which are currently artificially discriminated against.
- It would prevent one party dominating and so concentrating too much power in too few hands.
- It would make all votes of equal value.
- A multi-party system might result in more consensus policies.
- It would bring Britain into line with the rest of Europe.

15 Lessons about first-past-the-post from the 2010 general election include these:

- Though normally FPTP produces a clear winner, it can throw up a hung parliament and political uncertainty.
- The results exaggerate the scale of the largest party's support.
- It continues to show how much the Liberal Democrats are discriminated against.
- Small parties are excluded from power — only one small party, the Greens, won one seat.

16 The three main differences between insider and outsider pressure groups are these:

- Insiders have close links with government and Parliament, outsiders do not.
- Insiders are forced to behave more responsibly than outsiders.
- Insiders tend to rely on direct influence on government, outsiders rely more on mobilising public support and pressurising government in that way.

17 Explanations for a lack of clear distinction between parties and pressure groups include these:

- Some pressure groups put up candidates for election like parties — an example is the Right-to-Life Campaign.
- Some pressure groups, like UKIP, gradually turn themselves into parties.
- Some parties, like the BNP, have a narrow range of issues only, like pressure groups.

18 Methods of insiders and outsiders differ in a number of ways:

- Insiders tend to concentrate on lobbying, while outsiders concentrate more on direct action.
- Insiders act responsibly, while outsiders sometimes use civil disobedience.
- Outsiders pressurise government by demonstrating widespread support for their issues, whereas insiders tend to use rational argument and hard evidence to support their aims.

19 Choose your own pressure groups. Explain whether they have been successful in any of the following respects. Include an explanation of success.

- promoting friendly legislation
- preventing unfriendly legislation

- amending legislation to make it more friendly
- reversing government decisions or policies
- placing their issues high in public awareness and on the political agenda

The reasons why they have been successful might include one or some of these:

- They may have mobilised widespread public support.
- They may have mounted a well-organised, eye-catching campaign.
- They may have had access to considerable finance.
- They may have used celebrity support.
- They may have used insider status to influence decision makers.

20 The ways in which pressure groups are good for democracy include these:

- They help to disperse power and prevent accumulations of power in few hands.
- They protect the rights and interests of minorities.
- They educate and inform the public.
- They are a balance against the power of government.
- They give opportunities for healthy political participation.
- They help people to express their grievances democratically.
- They are important channels of communication between the people and government.